SOUND

CONNECTING STUDENTS TO SCIENCE SERIES

By

LAVERNE LOGAN

COPYRIGHT © 2003 Mark Twain Media, Inc.

ISBN 1-58037-251-1

Printing No. CD-1614

Mark Twain Media, Inc., Publishers
Distributed by Carson-Dellosa Publishing Company, Inc.

TABLE OF CONTENTS

INTRODUCTION TO THE SERIES

The Connecting Students to Science Series is designed for grades 5–8. This series will introduce the following topics: Simple Machines, Electricity and Magnetism, Rocks and Minerals, Atmosphere and Weather, Chemistry, Light and Color, The Solar System, and Sound. Each book will contain an introduction to the topic, naive concepts, inquiry activities, content integration, materials lists, children's literature connections, curriculum resources, assessment documents, and a bibliography.

Students will develop an understanding of the concepts and processes of science through the use of good scientific techniques. Students will be engaged in higher-level thinking skills while doing fun and interesting activities. All of the activities will be aligned with the National Science Education Standards and National Council of Teachers of Mathematics Standards.

This series is written for classroom teachers, parents, families, and students. The books in this series can be used as a full unit of study or as individual lessons to supplement existing textbooks or curriculum programs. Activities are designed to be pedagogically sound, hands-on, minds-on science activities that support the National Science Education Standards (NSES). Parents and students could use this series as an enhancement to what is being done in the classroom or as a tutorial at home. The procedures and content background are clearly explained in the introduction and within the individual activities. Materials used in the activities are commonly found in classrooms and homes.

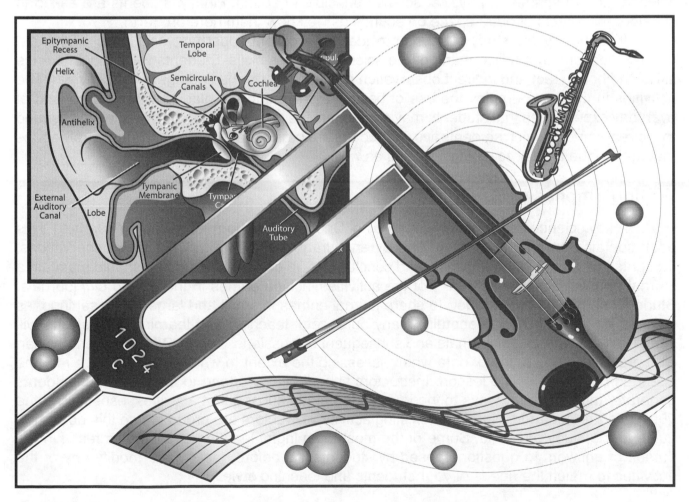

INTRODUCTION TO THE TOPIC AND MAJOR CONCEPTS

Interdisciplinary Applications

Welcome to the study of sound. Sounds are all around us and impact the daily lives of all students. Many students may not recognize the importance of sound in their daily lives. The goal of this book is to increase content knowledge of the science of sound and increase awareness of its importance in students' daily lives. To that end, the activities in this book also reflect an interdisciplinary approach to the study of sound. Students' everyday lives are not compartmentalized by subject disciplines. This study of sound seeks to actively capitalize on natural connections between subject disciplines. For example, music provides a natural context within which sound can be studied. Listening and speaking, two of the four major language arts skills, require the science of sound. Even our economy is greatly affected by sound, particularly in the forms of communication technologies, e.g., digital and analog transmission, music sales, radio and television, and other forms of mass communication.

Users of this book will also note natural connections between disciplines within science. For example, many animals (life science) have unique adaptations related to sound, which help them to survive and communicate, e.g., bats, owls, whales, etc. A fuller understanding of the science of sound can be achieved when studying sound within the context of the human ear and sense of hearing (life science). Geophysical features such as canyons and caves (earth science) create echoes, a physical science principle of sound. Finally, students are asked to consider the effects of outer space on sounds as we know them here on Earth.

In summary, the study of sound provides an excellent opportunity for hands-on, minds-on investigations that utilize many of the science process skills. Students will apply inference skills and both direct and indirect observation as they analyze the findings of the activities. The activities in this book employ the use of basic materials and are placed within the context of everyday experiences that students may encounter. The goal is to connect the science of sound to the real world in which students live. Instructors are urged to add interdisciplinary applications that are unique to their teaching contexts as well.

Writing Emphasis–*Sound Off!*

A key science process skill is recording. One important form of recording is writing. This book contains an emphasis on writing by encouraging students to write their observations, thoughts, questions, data, analysis, and conclusions. To do so, each student should maintain a journal entitled *"Sound Off!"* Many of the activities include entries in the *Sound Off!* journals. Students should be encouraged to share journal entries in small and large group settings, as dictated by the instructor. Hopefully, many purposeful teaching and learning discussions will stem from the *Sound Off!* journals and subsequent discussions. *Sound Off!* journal entries can also provide a rich source of data when assessing the extent to which students have met the intended objectives of the lesson. Instructors should keenly attend to the questions students generate and search for ways to incorporate them into subsequent activities, especially if the questions are not addressed in an existing activity. Instructors are urged to use this book as a guide to the study of sound. Some of the most meaningful learning experiences result in the pursuit of answers to questions posed by students. As before, feel free to modify any of the activities to match the needs of your students and teaching style.

NAIVE CONCEPTS AND TERMINOLOGY DEFINITIONS

Introduction: Our understanding of the natural world is directly related to commonly occurring experiences, including those that occur in and out of the science classroom. Sometimes the everyday descriptions of phenomena lead to concepts that are either incomplete or inaccurate. For example, students may only consider sound within the context of the sense of hearing. By providing experiences in which they can feel vibrations that produce sound energy, students may gain a more complete sensory view of the principles of sound. We may refer to our developing conception of the world and the way things work or the way life works as being in the process of development. In this way, some of our ideas may be naive. Some authors refer to these developing concepts as misconceptions. For the purpose of this resource, we will refer to them as naive ideas.

Naive Ideas Related to Sound

One area for potential naive conceptions is related to the terminology used. Many commonly used words have a specific and alternative meaning in science. A second area that may serve as a source for naive conceptions occurs when intuitive ideas gained through everyday experience are contrary to the more formal structure of scientific concepts.

Words that may serve as a source for confusion include:

Amplitude: the size of the sound wave; students may interchange frequency and amplitude.

Cochlea: located in the inner ear, a spiral-shaped, liquid-filled part of the ear in which sounds are converted into electrical signals that are then transmitted to the brain

Decibel: the unit of measure for the intensity/loudness of sound; labeled dB

Doppler effect: the change in the pitch of a sound as its source moves past a fixed point; students may not realize that the Doppler effect can occur when either the sound source or the listener is moving.

Eardrum: provides the entrance to the middle ear; consists of a lightly stretched membrane; students may be unaware that the eardrum can be damaged when exposed to sounds that are too loud.

Echoes: reflection of sound waves; students should be made aware of echoes that occur in natural geophysical formations and manmade structures, e.g., the side of their gymnasium.

3

Naive Concepts and Terminology Definitions (cont.)

Echolocation: a navigational system used by some animals as they send out sounds and interpret the reflection of sounds; used for locating food, defense, and general navigation. Students may be unaware of the number of animals that rely upon echolocation.

Frequency: the number of waves produced per unit of time; measured in hertz (Hz)

Infrasonic sound: waves that fall below normal human hearing range, e.g., less than 20 Hz

Interference: interaction of two sound waves that overlap; often classified as constructive interference (amplitude is increased by wave overlap) and destructive interference (amplitude is decreased by wave overlap)

Medium: matter necessary for sound waves to be transmitted; students may mistakenly assume that sound travels through a vacuum. Students may also assume that sound travels only through air, since that is how they normally hear sounds.

Middle ear: consists of the hammer, anvil, and stirrup; these work in conjunction to increase the size of the vibrations caused by sounds; students may not realize that the eardrum forms the entrance to the middle ear.

Outer ear: consists of the pinna and ear canal; its function is to collect sounds and direct them toward the middle and inner ear.

Pitch: frequency of the sound; how high or low the sound is perceived to be

Reflection: a wave bounces back after striking a surface; students may not be aware that sound waves reflect, since they are invisible.

Resonance: sound increasing when a vibrating object nears the natural frequency of another object

Sonar: acronym for **so**und **n**avigating **a**nd **r**anging; students may be unaware that some animals have this as their major navigation system.

Ultrasonic: sound waves that fall above normal human hearing range, e.g., greater than 20,000 Hz

Wave: disturbance in a medium that transmits energy; students may think of sound waves as transverse rather than longitudinal or compressional.

NATIONAL STANDARDS

NSES Content Standards (NRC, 1996)
National Research Council (1996). *National Science Education Standards.* Washington, D.C.: National Academy Press.

Unifying Concepts K–12
Systems, Order, and Organization
The natural and designed world is complex. Scientists and students learn to define small portions for the convenience of investigation. The units of investigation can be referred to as systems. A system is an organized group of related objects or components that form a whole. Systems can consist of machines.

Evidence, Models, and Explanation
The goal of this standard is to ...
- Recognize that evidence consists of observations and data upon which to base scientific explanations.
- Recognize that models have explanatory power.
- Recognize that scientific explanations incorporate existing scientific knowledge (laws, principles, theories, paradigms, models) and new evidence from observations, experiments, or models.
- Recognize that scientific explanations should reflect a rich scientific knowledge base, evidence of logic, higher levels of analysis, greater tolerance of criticism and uncertainty, and a clear demonstration of the relationship between logic, evidence, and current knowledge.

Change, Constancy, and Measurement
The goal of this standard is to ...
- Recognize that some properties of objects are characterized by constancy, including the speed of light, the charge of an electron, and the total mass plus energy of the universe.
- Recognize that changes might occur in the properties of materials, position of objects, motion, and form and function of systems.
- Recognize that changes in systems can be quantified.
- Recognize that measurement systems may be used to clarify observations.

Form and Function
The goal of this standard is to ...
- Recognize that the form of an object is frequently related to its use, operation, or function.
- Recognize that function frequently relies on form.
- Recognize that form and function apply to different levels of organization.
- Students should be able to explain function by referring to form, and to explain form by referring to function.

NATIONAL STANDARDS (CONT.)

NSES Content Standard A: Inquiry
- Abilities necessary to do scientific inquiry are to ...
  - Identify questions that can be answered through scientific investigations.
  - Design and conduct a scientific investigation.
  - Use appropriate tools and techniques to gather, analyze, and interpret data.
  - Develop descriptions, explanations, predictions, and models using evidence.
  - Think critically and logically to make relationships between evidence and explanations.
  - Recognize and analyze alternative explanations and predictions.
  - Communicate scientific procedures and explanations.
  - Use mathematics in all aspects of scientific inquiry.

- Understanding about inquiry means that ...
  - Different kinds of questions suggest different kinds of scientific investigations.
  - Current scientific knowledge and understanding guide scientific investigations.
  - Mathematics is important in all aspects of scientific inquiry.
  - Technology used to gather data enhances accuracy and allows scientists to analyze and quantify results of investigations.
  - Scientific explanations emphasize evidence, have logically consistent arguments, and use scientific principles, models, and theories.
  - Science advances through legitimate skepticism.
  - Scientific investigations sometimes result in new ideas and phenomena for study, generate new methods or procedures, or develop new technologies to improve data collection.

NSES Content Standard B: Properties and Changes of Properties in Matter 5–8

NSES Content Standard C: Structure and Function in Living Systems 5–8

NSES Content Standard C: Regulation and Behavior 5–8

NSES Content Standard D: Structure of the Earth System 5–8

NSES Content Standard D: Earth in the Solar System 5–8

NATIONAL STANDARDS (CONT.)

NSES Content Standard E: Science and Technology 5–8
- Abilities of Technological Design
  - Identify appropriate problems for technological design
  - Design a solution or product
  - Implement the proposed design
  - Evaluate completed technological designs or products
  - Communicate the process of technological design
- Understandings About Science and Technology
  - Scientific inquiry and technological design have similarities and differences
  - Many people in different cultures have made and continue to make contributions
  - Science and technology are reciprocal
  - Perfectly designed solutions do not exist
  - Technological designs have constraints
  - Technological solutions have intended benefits and unintended consequences

NSES Content Standard F: Science in Personal and Social Perspectives 5–8
- Science and technology in society mean that ...
  - Science influences society through its knowledge and world view.
  - Societal challenges often inspire questions for scientific research.
  - Technology influences society through its products and processes.
  - Scientists and engineers work in many different settings.
  - Science cannot answer all questions, and technology cannot solve all human problems.

NSES Content Standard G: History and Nature of Science 5–8
- Science as a human endeavor
  - Nature of science
  - Scientists formulate and test their explanations of nature using observation, experiments, and theoretical and mathematical models.
  - It is normal for scientists to differ with one another about interpretation of evidence and theory.
  - It is part of scientific inquiry for scientists to evaluate the results of other scientists' work.
- History of Science
  - Many individuals have contributed to the traditions of science.
  - Science has been and is practiced by different individuals in different cultures.
  - Tracing the history of science can show how difficult it was for scientific innovators to break through the accepted ideas of their time to reach the conclusions we now accept.

NATIONAL STANDARDS (CONT.)

Standards for Technological Literacy (STL) International Technology Education Association

International Technology Education Association (2000). *Standards for Technological Literacy.* Reston, VA: International Technology Education Association.

The Nature of Technology
Students will develop an understanding of the ...
1. Characteristics and scope of technology.
2. Core concepts of technology.
3. Relationships among technologies and the connections between technology and other fields of study.

Technology and Society
Students will develop an understanding of the ...
4. Cultural, social, economic, and political effects of technology.
5. Effects of technology on the environment.
6. Role of society in the development and use of technology.
7. Influence of technology on history.

Design
Students will develop an understanding of the ...
8. Attributes of design.
9. Engineering design.
10. Role of troubleshooting, research and development, invention and innovation, and experimentation in problem solving.

Abilities for a Technological World
Students will develop abilities to ...
11. Apply the design process.
12. Use and maintain technological products and systems.
13. Assess the impact of products and systems.

The Designed World
Students will develop an understanding of, and be able to select and use ...
14. Medical technologies.
15. Agricultural and related biotechnologies.
16. Energy and power technologies.
17. Information and communication technologies.
18. Transportation technologies.
19. Manufacturing technologies.
20. Construction technologies.

NATIONAL STANDARDS (CONT.)

Principles And Standards For School Mathematics (NCTM, 2000)
National Council of Teachers of Mathematics. (2000). *Principles and Standards for School Mathematics*. Reston, VA: National Council of Teachers of Mathematics.

Number and Operations
Students will be enabled to …
- Understand numbers, ways of representing numbers, relationships among numbers, and number systems.
- Understand meanings of operations and how they relate to one another.
- Compute fluently and make reasonable estimates.

Algebra
Students will be enabled to …
- Understand patterns, relations, and functions.
- Represent and analyze mathematical situations and structures using algebraic symbols.
- Use mathematical models to represent and understand quantitative relationships.
- Analyze change in various contexts.

Geometry
Students will be enabled to …
- Analyze characteristics and properties of two- and three-dimensional geometric shapes and develop mathematical arguments about geometric relationships.
- Specify locations and describe spatial relationships using coordinate geometry and other representational systems.
- Apply transformations and use symmetry to analyze mathematical situations.
- Use visualization, spatial reasoning, and geometric modeling to solve problems.

Measurement
Students will be enabled to …
- Understand measurable attributes of objects and the units, systems, and processes of measurement.
- Apply appropriate techniques, tools, and formulas to determine measurements.

Data Analysis and Probability
Students will be enabled to …
- Formulate questions that can be addressed with data and collect, organize, and display relevant data to answer them.
- Select and use appropriate statistical methods to analyze data.
- Develop and evaluate inferences and predictions that are based on data.
- Understand and apply basic concepts of probability.

SCIENCE PROCESS SKILLS

Introduction:

Science is organized curiosity, and an important part of this organization is the thinking skills or information processing skills. We ask the question "Why?" and then must plan a strategy for answering. In the process of answering our questions, we make and carefully record observations, make predictions, identify and control variables, measure, make inferences, and communicate our findings. Additional skills may be called upon, depending upon the nature of our questions. In this way, science is a verb, involving active manipulation of materials and careful thinking. Science is dependent upon language, math, and reading skills, as well as the specialized thinking skills associated with identifying and solving problems.

BASIC PROCESS SKILLS

Classifying: Grouping, ordering, arranging, or distributing objects, events, or information into categories based on properties or criteria, according to some method or system.

> **Example** – The skill is being demonstrated if the student is …
> Classifying the origin of various sounds, e.g., strings, air, percussion, combinations, etc.

Observing: Using the senses (or extensions of the senses) to gather information about an object or event.

> **Example** – The skill is being demonstrated if the student is …
> Describing sounds, both qualitatively and quantitatively, using the senses of hearing, touch, and sight.

Measuring: Using both standard and nonstandard measures or estimates to describe the dimensions of an object or event; making quantitative observations.

> **Example** – The skill is being demonstrated if the student is …
> Recording data regarding the time lag between a sound from its source and perception from a distance.

Inferring: Making an interpretation or conclusion based on reasoning to explain an observation.

> **Example** – The skill is being demonstrated if the student is …
> Inferring that sound is associated with vibrations as they feel and hear sounds caused by striking a tuning fork.

SCIENCE PROCESS SKILLS (CONT.)

Communicating: Communicating ideas through speaking or writing. Students may share the results of investigations, collaborate on solving problems, and gather and interpret data, both orally and in writing; using graphs, charts, and diagrams to describe data.

> **Example** – The skill is being demonstrated if the student is ...
> Describing an event or a set of observations. Participating in brainstorming and hypothesizing before an investigation. Formulating initial and follow-up questions in the study of a topic. Summarizing data, interpreting findings, and offering conclusions. Questioning or refuting previous findings.

Predicting: Making a forecast of future events or conditions in the context of previous observations and experiences.

> **Example** – The skill is being demonstrated if the student is ...
> Speculating what will happen to the pitch if a string on a musical instrument is shortened and/or lengthened.

Manipulating Materials: Handling or treating materials and equipment skillfully and effectively.

> **Example** – The skill is being demonstrated if the student is ...
> Designing and building devices that create sounds in which the pitch and volume can be varied.

Using Numbers: Applying mathematical rules or formulas to calculate quantities or determine relationships from basic measurements.

> **Example** – The skill is being demonstrated if the student is ...
> Calculating the relationship between time and distance when measuring the speed of sound.

Developing Vocabulary: Specialized terminology and unique uses of common words in relation to a given topic need to be identified and given meaning.

> **Example** – The skill is being demonstrated if the student is ...
> Using context clues, working definitions, glossaries or dictionaries, word structure (roots, prefixes, suffixes), and synonyms and antonyms to clarify meaning.

SCIENCE PROCESS SKILLS (CONT.)

Questioning: Questions serve to focus inquiry, determine prior knowledge, and establish purposes or expectations for an investigation. An active search for information is promoted when questions are used.

> **Example** – The skill is being demonstrated if the student is …
> Using what is already known about a topic or concept to formulate questions for further investigation; hypothesizing and predicting prior to gathering data; or formulating questions as new information is acquired.

Using Cues: Key words and symbols convey significant meaning in messages. Organizational patterns facilitate comprehension of major ideas. Graphic features clarify textual information.

> **Example** – The skill is being demonstrated if the student is …
> Listing or underlining words and phrases that carry the most important details or relating key words together to express a main idea or concept.

INTEGRATED PROCESS SKILLS

Creating Models: Displaying information by means of graphic illustrations or other multisensory representations.

> **Example** – The skill is being demonstrated if the student is …
> Designing and constructing models of the key parts of the human ear and how they interact in order to allow humans to hear.

Formulating Hypotheses: Stating or constructing a statement that is testable about what is thought to be the expected outcome of an experiment (based on reasoning).

> **Example** – The skill is being demonstrated if the student is …
> Creating a statement to be tested, such as "an increase in percussion will result in an increase in amplitude."

Generalizing: Drawing general conclusions from particulars.

> **Example** – The skill is being demonstrated if the student is …
> Concluding that sounds travel faster through solids than through liquids and gases.

SCIENCE PROCESS SKILLS (CONT.)

Identifying and Controlling Variables: Recognizing the characteristics of objects or factors in events that are constant or change under different conditions and that can affect an experimental outcome, keeping most variables constant while manipulating only one variable.

> **Example –** The skill is being demonstrated if the student is …
> Listing variables to hold constant while manipulating the force of percussion (See example hypothesis above.).

Defining Operationally: Stating how to measure a variable in an experiment, defining a variable according to the actions or operations to be performed on or with it.

> **Example –** The skill is being demonstrated if the student is …
> Defining the procedures for stop and start times of measuring echoes.

Recording and Interpreting Data: Collecting bits of information about objects and events that illustrate a specific situation; organizing and analyzing data that has been obtained, and drawing conclusions from it by determining apparent patterns or relationships in the data.

> **Example –** The skill is being demonstrated if the student is …
> Recording data (taking notes, making lists/outlines, recording numbers on charts/graphs, making tape recordings, taking photographs, writing numbers of results of observations/ measurements) from observations to determine the differences between human hearing and that of various animals, particularly those that rely upon echolocation.

Making Decisions: Identifying alternatives and choosing a course of action from among alternatives, after basing the judgment for the selection on justifiable reasons.

> **Example –** The skill is being demonstrated if the student is …
> Designing and creating a musical instrument that aligns with one of the three major classifications of sound, e.g., percussion, strings, wind.

Experimenting: Being able to conduct an experiment, including asking an appropriate question, stating a hypothesis, identifying and controlling variables, operationally defining those variables, designing a "fair" experiment, and interpreting the results of an experiment.

> **Example –** The skill is being demonstrated if the student is …
> Formulating a researchable question, identifying and controlling variables, including a manipulated and responding variable, collecting and analyzing data, drawing conclusions, and formulating new questions as a result of the conclusions.

Name: _____ Date: _____

PRELIMINARY ACTIVITY I: QUICK-WRITE—SOUND

Prior to the start of the unit, help students construct *Sound Off!* journals to be used throughout the activities. Basic journals can easily be made by folding 10–15 sheets of 11 x 8.5-inch, lined notebook paper in half (top to bottom). Similarly, fold one piece of construction paper for use as a cover. Staple along the crease 2–3 times. Encourage students to entitle the journals and add their names. Students may wish to decorate the cover prior to the activities, and/or add illustrations of what they have learned as the activities are completed. In either case, students should bring the *Sound Off!* journal to class daily.

As a preliminary activity, ask students to write everything they know and believe to be true about sound and all matters related to sound in the *Sound Off!* journal. Give them ample time to construct these essays; allow them to include illustrations, diagrams, etc., particularly for low-ability students. To conclude the essay, instruct students to list questions that they have about sound.

Option:

In place of a free-response essay, instructors may wish to alter this assignment by providing guiding questions to which students should respond. Some examples may include:
1) What causes sounds?
2) What are the characteristics of sound?
3) In what ways do sounds vary?
4) What makes sounds different?
5) Why are sounds important in nature?
6) How do humans hear sounds?
7) Why are sounds important in our daily lives?

The purpose of this activity is threefold:
1. The essay will provide a unique perspective of any misconceptions regarding sound that students may have. It is vital that instructors examine the pre-existing perceptions that students hold. Please remember, any obvious misconceptions must be addressed throughout the study of sound, even if they are not addressed by any of the activities in this book.
2. The essay provides instructors with insight when making key instructional decisions, e.g., prioritize the order of lessons/concepts, examine current levels of knowledge and understanding, pacing and transitions.
3. The essay provides a nice assessment opportunity. Essays can be consulted and altered as new information is learned throughout the lessons/activities. Students may discover flaws in their original thinking. As time allows, be sure to provide opportunities to periodically review the essays and address what was originally thought. Perhaps students will wish to edit this document with another color of writing tool to display changes in thinking and levels of understanding.

Name: _____ Date: _____

PRELIMINARY ACTIVITY II: SOUNDS IN OUR WORLD

This preliminary activity is designed to measure students' awareness levels of sounds in the world around them. All data in this activity should be recorded in the *Sound Off!* journals. Instruct students to sit quietly and create a list of all of the distinct sounds they hear. Beside or beneath each sound, instruct students to add words that describe the sound listed without using the sound itself. For example, if students listed a car passing by, they should not use the word car, but rather adjectives that describe the sound(s) the car made as it passed by. Students will readily recognize that this endeavor is not as easy as it first appears.

Ideally, the activity should be completed in 10–15 minutes, both indoors and outdoors (keep separate lists). The instructor may wish to record both settings for later reference and assistance. Students may wish to add to their lists upon hearing the taped replay. Encourage students to remember these lists, as they will re-visit the lists within the first several activities.

Encourage students to compare and contrast their lists. You may wish to have students announce only the describing words while others guess the origin of the sound. As a class, discuss the differences between the various sounds. Record any questions that arise as a result of the preliminary activity. Use these as the basis for further investigation either during one of the activities to come or in the inquiry activity near the end of the book (See Independent Investigation.).

As an extension to promote parental involvement, ask students to speculate how the lists would differ if they were to do this activity outdoors, at night. Offer students extra credit or bonus points for repeating the activity at home with parents/guardians and/or siblings.

Name: _____ Date: _____

STUDENT INQUIRY ACTIVITY 1: WHAT IS SOUND?

Topic: Sound—Vibrations and Waves

Introductory Statement:

Sounds are vibrations and can be considered a form of energy. In this activity, you will characterize sound and become more aware of its importance in our daily lives.

NSES Content Standard B: Transfer of Energy

Energy is a property of many substances and is associated with heat, light, electricity, mechanical motion, sound, nuclei, and the nature of a chemical. Energy is transferred in many ways.

NSES Content Standard A: Understandings About Scientific Inquiry

Different kinds of questions suggest different kinds of scientific investigations. Some investigations involve observing and describing objects, organisms, or events; some involve collecting specimens; some involve experiments; some involve discovery of new objects and phenomena; and some involve making models.

Science Skills and Concepts:
- Students will identify sounds as a series of vibrations.
- Students will recognize sound waves as a form of energy.
- Students will infer that sound can be felt and heard.

Materials/Safety Concerns:

Sound Off! journal
Variety of tuning forks
Ping pong balls
Water and cups
Heavy-duty earplugs (hearing protectors)
Salt
Large balloons
String
Rulers
A Slinky™
Masking tape
Empty tin cans
Rubber bands

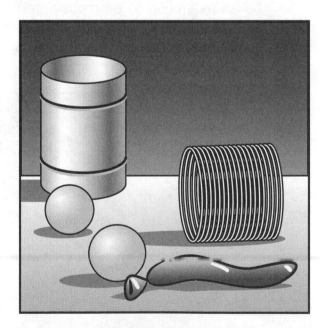

Content Background:

Sounds are vibrations in the form of waves. Waves are most easily demonstrated in a liquid; however, these are transverse waves that move in a direction perpendicular to the source of the disturbance. Sound waves are longitudinal or compressional waves. As an object vibrates, it compresses the surrounding air molecules (in a spherical pattern), which, in turn, compress the air molecules next to them, and so on. The compressed air molecules are followed by a brief

Name: _____ Date: _____

STUDENT INQUIRY ACTIVITY 1: WHAT IS SOUND? (CONT.)

period of less compressed air molecules. This is known as **rarefaction**, or rarified air. This pattern continues as long as the original disturbance continues to vibrate. Many sources may demonstrate waves by dropping water into a pan and observing the waves as they move to the outside of the pan. While sound shares some of the characteristics of transverse waves, students should come to recognize sound as compressional waves. These waves are also known as longitudinal because they travel in the direction of the disturbance (outwardly).

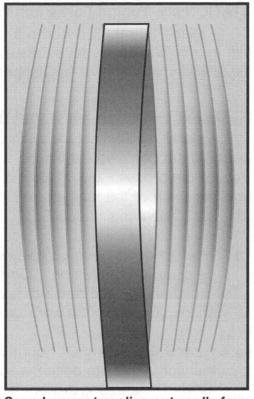

Sound waves traveling outwardly from the source.

Procedures

1. Arrange the room into station format representing four work areas entitled: Tuning Forks and Ping Pong Balls; Tuning Forks and Salt; Tuning Forks and Water; Tuning Forks and You. For the purposes of consistency, announce that the source of sound is held constant (always the tuning fork). Discuss proper care, use, and handling of the tuning forks. Instruct students to strike the tuning forks on relatively soft surfaces only, e.g., the lower palm or a soft-soled shoe.

2. Create instruction cards for each station, to reflect the directions contained on the Exploration/Data collection sheets. It may be useful to have several sets of materials at each station, especially if class size is large. All predictions, observations, and explanations should be recorded in the *Sound Off!* journals. The instructions should reflect the following:

STATION A – Tuning Forks and Ping Pong Balls

Tape a 25 cm length of string to a ping pong ball; grasp the end of the string and hold it out in front of you so that the ping pong ball hangs down. Predict and record what will happen if you strike the tuning fork and place it next to the ping-pong ball so that it barely touches. Try it! Record your observations, and explain why you believe this happened.

STATION B – Tuning Forks and Salt

Cut off the stem of a large balloon. Stretch the balloon open and place it across the top of a tin can and pull it tight, so the balloon is level across the top of the can. Secure the balloon by placing a strong rubber band around the top of the tin can and stretched balloon. Sprinkle salt onto the stretched balloon. Predict and record what will happen if you strike the tuning fork and hold it just above the surface of the balloon. Try it! Record your observations and explain why you believe this happened.

Name: _____ Date: _____

STUDENT INQUIRY ACTIVITY **1**: WHAT IS SOUND? (CONT.)

STATION C – Tuning Forks and Water

Place 50 mL of water in a cup. Predict and record what will happen if you strike the tuning fork and gently touch the surface of the water. Try it! Record your observations and explain why you believe this happened.

STATION D – Tuning Forks and You

Carefully disinfect the tuning fork by rubbing it with an alcohol swab. Predict and record what will happen if you strike the tuning fork and gently touch it to your opposite index finger. Repeat the process, only gently touch it to your lower lip. Repeat the process, only this time, hold the base of the tuning fork just behind your ear. Record your observations, and explain why you believe this happened.

3. After students have completed the tasks at all of the stations, discuss the findings and determine conclusions. Compare and contrast the predictions, observations, and explanations recorded by the students. Try to reach consensus on generalizations about sound/vibrations that were made as a result of the activities.

4. Review the *Sound Off!* journal entries from *Preliminary Activity II*. Ask students to share the words used to describe sounds they heard. Perhaps one or more students will have alluded to vibrating or vibrations. If not, introduce the word and inquire about its meaning. Ask students to think about how vibration might be related to sound, especially in light of the station activities.

5. Review the *Sound Off!* journal entries from *Preliminary Activity II*. Check to see if any students alluded to the word "wave" in their descriptive words lists. This will not likely be the case. Demonstrate compressional waves by using a Slinky™ on a long table. Have a student stretch the Slinky™ to one end of the table while you hold on to the other end.

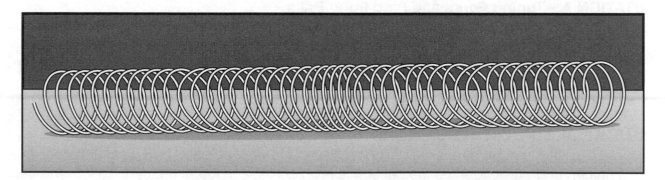

Gather roughly a quarter of the Slinky™ by pulling it together and then suddenly letting it go while you are still holding on to the very end. Students will be able to see a compressional, or longitudinal, wave surge through the Slinky™. Careful observers will also notice the reflection when the energy reaches the end of the Slinky™, as it bounces back.

Name: _____ Date: _____

STUDENT INQUIRY ACTIVITY 1: WHAT IS SOUND? (CONT.)

Achieve another excellent demonstration of compressional waves by lining students up in a single-file line, roughly one arm's length apart. Start a "disturbance" vibration at the rear of the line by lightly tapping the shoulder of the last student, who in turn leans forward and lightly taps the student in front of him/her, etc. Have students take turns watching (from the side) the wave surge through the line. The demonstration can be extended to include echoes, by declaring that the student at the front of the line represents a wall. When tapped, he/she can turn around and return the tap, sending the echo wave back through the line.

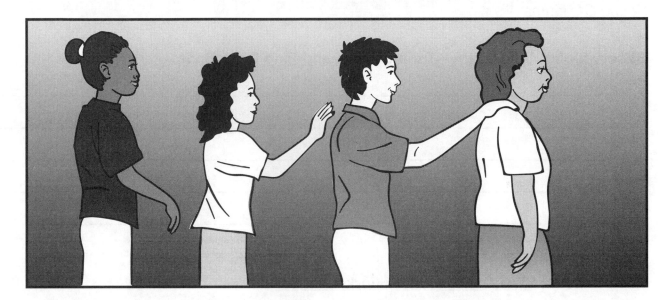

6. Discuss the importance of the vibrations caused by the original disturbance. Ask students why the sound waves eventually dissipate. Be sure to conclude that the compressional waves are latent and that we can only see the effects of them. Cite a real-world application of earthquakes, (e.g., although we can't directly see the waves created by earthquakes, we certainly can experience the effects of them!) Another appropriate application of latent energy is that of wind; we can only see the effects of wind.

7. Return to the stations and allow students to experience the tuning forks once again. Encourage free response in the *Sound Off!* journals regarding observations of vibrations and compressional waves.

8. Encourage students to illustrate their understanding of sound vibrations and waves on the cover of the *Sound Off!* journals. Suggest that they conserve space, as additional concepts will be added throughout the activities. Students can utilize both the inside and outside of the front and back covers for illustrations throughout the activities.

Name: _____ Date: _____

STUDENT INQUIRY ACTIVITY **1**: WHAT IS SOUND? (CONT.)

Exploration/Data Collection

(((VIBRATIONS!!!)))

Carefully follow the directions at each station. Record your observations either below or in your *Sound Off!* journal.

Observations: <u>STATION A – Tuning Forks and Ping Pong Balls</u>

_____

_____

_____

_____

_____

Observations: <u>STATION B – Tuning Forks and Salt</u>

_____

_____

_____

_____

_____

Observations: <u>STATION C – Tuning Forks and Water</u>

_____

_____

_____

_____

_____

Name: _____ Date: _____

STUDENT INQUIRY ACTIVITY **1**: WHAT IS SOUND? (CONT.)

Observations: <u>STATION D – Tuning Forks and You</u>

_____

_____

_____

_____

_____

Conclusions:

_____

_____

_____

_____

_____

Summary/What to Look For:
1. To what extent did students accurately describe vibrations and their relationship to sound?
2. To what extent did students infer sound as a form of energy?
3. To what extent did students identify the senses used to detect sound?
4. To what extent were students able to generalize the characteristics of sound to real-world applications?

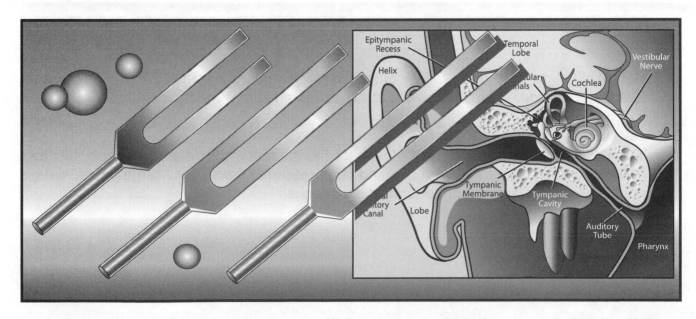

Name: _____ Date: _____

STUDENT INQUIRY ACTIVITY **1**: WHAT IS SOUND? (CONT.)

Discussion Questions/Assessment:

1. Review your observations from each station. Indicate which senses were used to identify sound.

   _____

   _____

   _____

   _____

   _____

   _____

2. True or False? Sound is a form of energy. Explain your reasoning.

   _____

   _____

   _____

   _____

3. Describe the meaning of the word *latent;* explain how it applies to sound.

   _____

   _____

   _____

   _____

4. Return to the original sound essay completed in *Preliminary Activity I*. Encourage students to edit and/or add information to the essay, using a different writing instrument.

Extension/Real-World Application:

1. Think of what happened at each station and in the follow-up class discussion. List any real-world applications of vibrations and compressional waves you can think of. Where might you see, feel, and/or hear similar experiences?

Name: _____ Date: _____

STUDENT INQUIRY ACTIVITY 2 : WHAT CAUSES SOUNDS?

Topic: Sound—Origin of Sounds

Introductory Statement:
Earlier, you learned about the characteristics of sound. In this activity, you will discover the various sources of sounds. Think about the key question: How are sounds made?

NSES Content Standard B: Transfer of Energy
Energy is a property of many substances and is associated with heat, light, electricity, mechanical motion, sound, nuclei, and the nature of a chemical. Energy is transferred in many ways.

NSES Content Standard E: Science and Technology
- Abilities of Technological Design
  - Identify appropriate problems for technological design
  - Design a solution or product
  - Implement the proposed design
  - Evaluate completed technological designs or products
  - Communicate the process of technological design

Science Skills and Concepts:
- Students will infer three major causes of sounds: percussion, strings vibrating, and air.
- Students will classify sounds according to their origin.
- Students will identify relationships between characteristics of sounds and their origins.

Materials/Safety Concerns:
Sound Off! journal
Various types of musical instruments, e.g., tambourine, recorder, guitar, snare drum, whistle, kazoo, maracas, triangle, etc.
Blindfolds, one for each pair of students
As per student request, various materials needed to create basic musical instruments, e.g., string, rubber bands, small boxes, straws, paper clips, toothpicks, etc.
Internet access
Various reference materials regarding music and orchestra, e.g., encyclopedia, almanac, etc.

Content Background:
     Earlier, students learned that sound is energy transferred in longitudinal waves. Sound can be characterized as vibrations or disturbances in a medium. This lesson seeks to narrow the source of vibrations by classifying the cause of most sounds into three major groups: vibrations caused by percussion or two objects coming into contact with each other; sounds produced by strings that vibrate; and vibrations produced by moving air. Although these classifications entail most sounds, it is important

Name: _____ Date: _____

STUDENT INQUIRY ACTIVITY 2 : WHAT CAUSES SOUNDS? (CONT.)

to understand that many sounds are produced by a combination of these factors. For example, the human voice represents a combination of air moving across strings within the voice box. Therefore, these major classifications of sound sources should only be used as general guides.

The very nature of the three major classifications of sound sources is the essence of music. One only needs to consider the instruments represented in an orchestra to easily identify

each classification or combination. Students should attend to the idea that the study of sound is inherently the study of music as well. For the purposes of this lesson, focus on the origin of sounds; a later lesson will delve into the various ways in which sounds (in music) vary, e.g., pitch.

In an effort to model an interdisciplinary approach to teaching and learning, plan to involve the music teacher while investigating the science of sound. Team together to help clarify the relationship between the science of sound and music. Obviously, preplanning is necessary, but whenever possible, invite the music teacher into science class. In return, attend music class with your students. Be sure to clarify your science objectives and curricular needs and encourage the music teacher to clarify his/her music objectives and curricular needs. Together, search for connections in which the two overlap.

Finally, this lesson does not take into account sounds that are produced electronically (digitally). Some music instructors may wish to broach this topic by demonstrating and explaining a synthesizer and how it operates.

Procedures:

1. Invite students to individually generate five unique sounds that are detectable with the human ear and are repeatable. Examples may include tapping two pencils together, erasing, plucking a shoestring, or blowing on a pinwheel. (*Management Tip:* You may wish to consider ground rules regarding volume and behavior. For example, some may take umbrage at fingernails on a chalkboard!)

2. Assign students to work in pairs. One student should be blindfolded; he/she is to guess the sounds made by the other student. Each sound may be repeated no more than two times (three total) before the guess must be made. For hints, students may ask three yes/no questions of the person creating the sound. The person who makes the sound should record the guess of the blindfolded student. Roles should be reversed; repeat the activity.

Name: _____ Date: _____

STUDENT INQUIRY ACTIVITY **2** : WHAT CAUSES SOUNDS? (CONT.)

3. Review the content learned from the previous activity, e.g., sound as energy transferred in waves; vibrations. In a large-group format, encourage students to share sample sound ideas they created. List the sounds on the board. Pose the question, "What caused these sounds?" Focus the students' attention on the behavior undertaken to create the sounds. As a class, try to generate categories into which the sound sources would fit. Accept the categories put forth by the class; however, also look for an opportunity to introduce these classifications (percussion, strings, air, specific combinations). This opportunity may become obvious, especially if one or more students reference musical sounds. Be sure to identify the concept of vibration as it applies to each classification.

4. In pairs, have students classify the remaining sounds on each of their lists. Each pair should then share their results with one other pair of students, in order to check for accuracy. Encourage students to explain and defend their classifications. Any disagreements (this is a good thing!) can be brought up for discussion in large-group format.

5. Challenge students to use music reference materials and Internet resources to create a list of the major instrument groups in an orchestra. Explain that you do not have access to the expensive musical instruments; however, you do have some less expensive instruments that rely upon many of the same sound principles.

6. Allow students to experiment with the musical instruments, carefully identifying classification (See earlier classifications scheme.) into which each instrument fits.

7. Challenge students to create a musical instrument of their own that creates sound according to one of the major classifications of sound sources. Examples may include a series of rubber bands stretched over a small, open box or a loaf pan; a homemade snare drum using an oatmeal box; a recorder using straws; a triangle using paper clips, etc. Encourage students to be creative as they design, build, test, and redesign the instruments. These will also be used in a later lesson. Suggest that students use the resident music teacher as an expert consultant on the project.

8. Encourage students to share and demonstrate their musical instruments with the class. Require them to explain which of the three major classifications is represented, along with a rationale.

Name: _____ Date: _____

STUDENT INQUIRY ACTIVITY 2 : WHAT CAUSES SOUNDS? (CONT.)

Exploration/Data Collection:

1. Think about ways to create five unique, yet repeatable sounds. Do not share this information with anyone else. Record your plans for making the sounds in your *Sound Off!* journal.

2. Listening carefully, guess the sounds made by your partner. You may ask your partner no more than three yes/no questions about each sound. He/she may only repeat the sound two times (total of three). Since you are blindfolded and can't see to write, have your partner record your guesses on your paper below:

My Sound Predictions

Sound #1: _____

Sound #2: _____

Sound #3: _____

Sound #4: _____

Sound #5: _____

3. After all guesses have been made and recorded, remove the blindfold and have the student demonstrate the sound. If the guess is inaccurate, record the correct sound next to the guess.

4. Consider the accuracy of your guesses. In your *Sound Off!* journal, record what factors caused you to be in error, and what factors helped you to correctly identify the sound. Record your thoughts about what would help you be more accurate if you were to try this again in the future.

5. Working together, classify your sounds according to their sources; see the main classifications on the chalkboard. Write the classification beside each actual sound on the table from *My Sound Predictions*.

6. Design and build a musical instrument capable of producing sound according to one of the major classifications: percussion, strings, air, and specific combination. Describe and sketch your design in your *Sound Off!* journal and seek approval from your instructor before beginning construction. In your plans, include which major classification is represented and why. Be prepared to explain your design, demonstrate your instrument for the class, and identify the major classification and why it fits into that classification. Good luck!

Name: _____ Date: _____

STUDENT INQUIRY ACTIVITY 2 : WHAT CAUSES SOUNDS? (CONT.)

Summary/What to Look For:

1. To what extent did students accurately state the three major classifications of sound sources?
2. To what extent did students correctly classify the sound and its source?
3. To what extent did students infer the relationship between vibration and three major classifications of sound sources?

Discussion Questions/Assessment:

1. Return to the indoor and outdoor sound lists created in *Preliminary Activity II*. Individually, have students classify the source of each of the sounds and explain how vibrations are present in each.

2. Have students return to their original essays they wrote about everything they believe to be true about sound. Encourage them to use a different writing instrument to edit anything they wish to change. They can add any new information from these activities about which they feel confident.

3. Encourage students to illustrate their understanding of major classifications of sound sources on the cover of the *Sound Off!* journals.

Extension/Real-World Application:

Encourage students to record and list evidence of the major classifications of sounds at their homes and/or during a favorite television show.

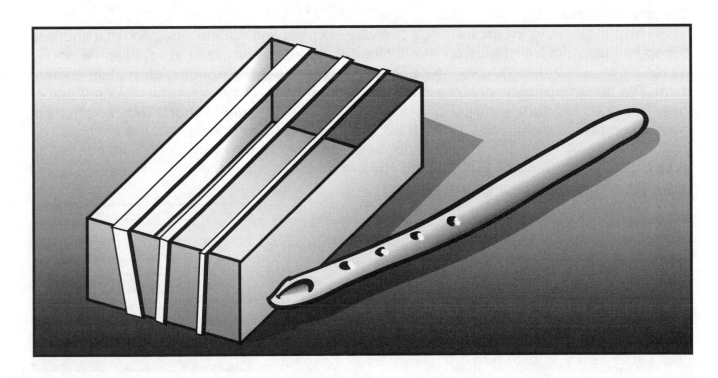

Name: _____ Date: _____

STUDENT INQUIRY ACTIVITY **3**: IN WHAT WAYS DO SOUNDS VARY?

Topic: Sound—Volume and Pitch

Introductory Statement:

So far, you have learned about what sound is and three major causes of sound. In this lesson, you will discover how sounds are different and what causes them to vary.

NSES Content Standard B: Transfer of Energy

Energy is a property of many substances and is associated with heat, light, electricity, mechanical motion, sound, nuclei, and the nature of a chemical. Energy is transferred in many ways.

Science Skills and Concepts:

- Students will cite two ways in which sounds can vary.
- Students will differentiate between pitch and volume.
- Students will infer the relationship between amplitude/intensity and volume.
- Students will infer the relationship between frequency of vibration and pitch or tone.
- Students will devise ways to vary pitch and volume on musical instruments.

Materials/Safety Concerns:

Sound Off! journal

Musical instruments constructed in the previous lesson

Reference materials related to musical scales

Internet access

Content Background:

Two major ways in which sounds can vary are pitch and volume. The pitch of a sound is dependent upon its **frequency**, or the number of waves per unit of time (cycles). As sound waves move outward, they have the same pitch/frequency as the vibrating object that created them. The sound's **pitch** is determined by the number of times the object vibrates per unit of time. This is also known as the period of vibration. Pitch is measured in **hertz (Hz)**; one hertz is equal to one wave per second. Since most sound waves travel considerably faster than one wave per second, humans have the ability to hear sounds in the ranges of 20–20,000 Hz. In essence, the faster something vibrates, the higher the pitch or frequency. Students may recognize this more commonly as the tone of a sound.

Volume is a second way to vary sounds. This is accomplished by increasing the intensity of the vibration, or greater energy transfer. Increasing the intensity of a sound is accomplished by increasing the **amplitude** (height of the wave) of the sound waves. Note that it is possible to increase the volume of a sound while maintaining the same frequency. Volume and pitch are therefore, very different, yet related concepts. For example, you could strike a small drum at a given frequency and achieve a given level of volume

Name: _____ Date: _____

STUDENT INQUIRY ACTIVITY 3 : IN WHAT WAYS DO SOUNDS VARY? (CONT.)

(measured in decibels). Next, you could strike the small drum at the same frequency but twice as hard, thereby increasing the volume, but maintaining the frequency. In essence, to increase the volume, increased energy transfer must occur.

In this lesson, students will investigate ways in which to alter both the pitch and volume of the musical instruments they constructed in the previous lesson. With the assistance of the music teacher, students can recognize the standard pitches universally accepted by musicians. Perhaps it will be possible to roughly "tune" some of the instruments.

Procedures:

1. Briefly review the content learned to date: the nature of waves and vibrations, the three major classifications of sound sources, examples of these classifications that occur naturally (both indoors and outdoors), and examples of handmade instruments that also fit one of these classifications. Entertain and record any questions students may have through this point in the study of sound. Although you may wish to deal with the questions directly at this time, another option would be to retain these questions as possible investigations during a later inquiry activity.

2. Have students obtain their musical instruments made in the previous lesson; make sure each is in proper working order. Set the instruments aside so students will not be tempted to play them during the class discussion.

3. Entertain ideas from students when posed with the question, "What are some ways in which you could vary the sound your musical instrument makes?" List these ideas on the chalkboard or on chart paper. Students will likely tell you what they can do (physically) to the instrument to vary the sound. Lead the discussion to introduce that what you do to the instrument affects either the pitch or volume. For example, they may suggest shortening one of the strings; this would result in a change in pitch. From the students' responses, classify the list to include those modifications that would likely affect volume and pitch. Please note that students may have various descriptions, e.g., loudness and tone; accept these as well.

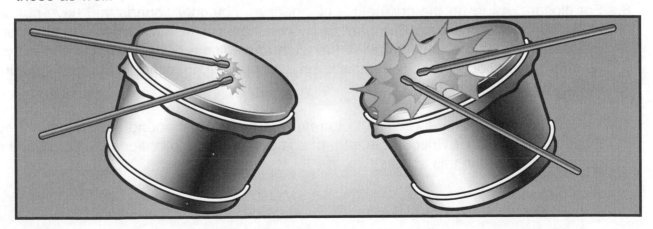

Name: _____ Date: _____

STUDENT INQUIRY ACTIVITY 3 : IN WHAT WAYS DO SOUNDS VARY? (CONT.)

4. Further challenge students to actually make the modifications to their instruments. Require them to narrate a plan to alter both the pitch and volume of their instrument in their *Sound Off!* journal. As before, the plan must be approved before modifications begin. This time, they must make the case and seek approval from at least two other students who have a musical instrument in another sound source classification. For example, a person with a string instrument must ask students from either a percussion, air, or combination group. The approving student must initial the plans in the *Sound Off!* journal, and may be called upon to defend his/her approval. This is designed to increase student-to-student interaction as well as to increase exposure to other sound source classifications and pitch/volume applications. As before, the music teacher would make a fine pitch and volume consultant.

5. Require students to journal about their progress as they work. It is one thing to devise a plan of action, and quite another to get the plan to work. Ask students to document and sketch trials and failures, adjustments, problems encountered, the thinking process, interactions with reference materials, etc. This narrative will not only sharpen students' abilities to communicate, but will also provide a rich source of data for assessment. Students will most likely need to be reminded to journal as they work.

6. After students have had ample time to work, ask them to return to the fellow student approvers and demonstrate their wares. Urge them to share the contents of their journals and discuss their findings collectively. Students may find that others had similar problems and struggles; they will also observe unique ideas that they may not have previously considered.

7. Call the attention of the class. Announce a new challenge: This time, alter the pitch and volume in the opposite direction! For example, many students may have only increased the volume; they must now decrease the volume. Some students may have generated a lower pitch or tone; they must now seek a higher pitch. As before, this should be documented in the *Sound Off!* journals. Encourage large-group sharing of the results.

8. For closure, return to the original list of indoor and outdoor sounds that have not been classified by sound source. Compare and contrast the pitches and volumes of the sounds. Discuss what factors may influence the pitch and volume of these sounds. Identify the source of vibration and discuss how it may vary (pitch). Identify factors that impact the intensity of the sound and how it may vary.

9. Provide an opportunity for students to return to the original sound essays generated in *Preliminary Activity I*. Encourage them to edit and/or add applications of information and concepts learned in this activity.

Name: _____ Date: _____

STUDENT INQUIRY ACTIVITY **3** : IN WHAT WAYS DO SOUNDS VARY? (CONT.)

Exploration/Data Collection:

Merry Music Makers!

1. In your *Sound Off!* journal, detail plans to alter the pitch and volume of your instrument. Be sure to provide plenty of instructions and details; pretend another student will carry out your plans and needs to know exactly what to do and in what order.

2. You have just received an urgent memo from the Sound Commissioner; please read carefully:

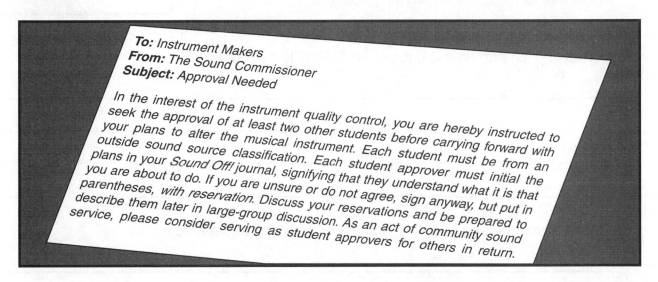

To: Instrument Makers
From: The Sound Commissioner
Subject: Approval Needed

In the interest of the instrument quality control, you are hereby instructed to seek the approval of at least two other students before carrying forward with your plans to alter the musical instrument. Each student must be from an outside sound source classification. Each student approver must initial the plans in your *Sound Off!* journal, signifying that they understand what it is that you are about to do. If you are unsure or do not agree, sign anyway, but put in parentheses, with reservation. Discuss your reservations and be prepared to describe them later in large-group discussion. As an act of community sound service, please consider serving as student approvers for others in return.

3. Extend the activity to include plans to complete the opposite version of what you have just done. For example, if you designed plans to increase the volume and heighten the pitch, your new task is to decrease the volume and lower the pitch and vice versa.

   As before, record your plans and observations in the *Sound Off!* journal. Record the details carefully, as you may be asked to share your results with others. Because of your original success, no student approval is needed for your plans, although you may consult with others.

4. Return to the original essay you wrote about everything you believe to be true about sound. Using a different writing instrument, edit anything you wish to change. Add any new information from these activities about which you feel confident.

Name: _____ Date: _____

STUDENT INQUIRY ACTIVITY **3** : IN WHAT WAYS DO SOUNDS VARY? (CONT.)

Summary/What to Look For:

1. To what extent did students identify two major ways in which to vary sound?
2. To what extent were students able to alter musical instruments to increase/decrease volume?
3. To what extent were students able to alter musical instruments to increase/decrease pitch?
4. To what extent were students able to infer the relationship between pitch and frequency?
5. To what extent were students able to infer the relationship between amplitude/intensity and volume?

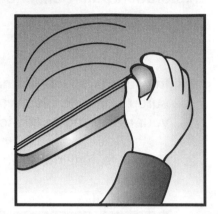

Discussion Questions/Assessment:

1. What is pitch and how is it increased? How is it decreased?

   _____

   _____

   _____

   _____

2. What is volume and how is it increased? How is it decreased?

   _____

   _____

   _____

   _____

3. What is the relationship between the pitch of a sound and its frequency? Please provide a real-world example.

   _____

   _____

   _____

   _____

   _____

Name: _____ Date: _____

STUDENT INQUIRY ACTIVITY 3: IN WHAT WAYS DO SOUNDS VARY? (CONT.)

4. What is the relationship between the amplitude/intensity of a sound and its volume? Please provide a real-world example.

_____
_____
_____
_____
_____

5. Quite often, we hear sounds that fade out until we can no longer hear them. What are two reasons this might happen? Please provide real-world examples for each reason.

_____
_____
_____
_____
_____

6. Encourage students to illustrate their understanding of how sounds can vary on the cover of the *Sound Off!* journals.

7. Review your first three activities related to sounds. Generate a list of questions that you have regarding any of the concepts, ideas, and activities from the first three lessons. You may wish to list things you would like to investigate further. There will be opportunities to follow up on this list later in the study of sound.

_____
_____
_____
_____
_____
_____

Name: _____ Date: _____

STUDENT INQUIRY ACTIVITY 3: IN WHAT WAYS DO SOUNDS VARY? (CONT.)

Extension/Real-World Application:

1. As time allows (or for early finishers), formulate a mini-band committee to take on the task of recruiting instrument makers and players to perform the school song. Encourage the help of the music teacher, especially if there is a need for tuning instruments.

2. For students interested in race cars, provide a tape of the Indianapolis 500 and/or Brickyard 500. Inquire about the difference in pitch and volume as the cars pass by the camera. Urge students to research, discover, explain, and demonstrate the Doppler effect.

Name: _____ Date: _____

STUDENT INQUIRY ACTIVITY **4** : IN WHAT WAYS DO SOUNDS TRAVEL?

Topic: Sound—Movement of Sound

Introductory Statement:

     In this lesson, you will apply what you have learned about vibrations and waves as you discover how sound travels. You will also observe how sound travels through solids, liquids, and gases.

NSES Content Standard B: Transfer of Energy

Energy is a property of many substances and is associated with heat, light, electricity, mechanical motion, sound, nuclei, and the nature of a chemical. Energy is transferred in many ways.

NSES Content Standard A: Understandings About Scientific Inquiry

Different kinds of questions suggest different kinds of scientific investigations. Some investigations involve observing and describing objects, organisms, or events; some involve collecting specimens; some involve experiments; some involve discovery of new objects and phenomena; and some involve making models.

Science Skills and Concepts:
- Students will infer that sound travels.
- Students will infer that a medium is needed for sound to travel.
- Students will identify differences in the speed of sound in varying mediums.
- Students will synthesize the relationship of vibrations, longitudinal waves, and the speed of sound.
- Students will compare the speed of sound to the speed of light.
- Students will apply concepts of sound travel to solve a communication problem.

Materials/Safety Concerns:

Sound Off! journal

A small wind-up clock or wristwatch (waterproof, if possible)	Gallon-sized resealable plastic bags
Large wooden blocks	String
Access to a long wooden conference table	Tuning forks
Tin cans	Stethoscope

Metal spoons/forks/knives
Large fish tank or glass container
Thump sticks or two flat boards with handles
Access to a large, open, outdoor area, e.g., football field, open meadow area
Track starter gun (if available)
A 9-volt lantern or beacon

Name: _____ Date: _____

STUDENT INQUIRY ACTIVITY 4 : IN WHAT WAYS DO SOUNDS TRAVEL? (CONT.)

Content Background:

Sound is characterized as a transfer of energy as a result of a disturbance. Sound travels in longitudinal or compressional waves. Since sound is dependent upon the compression and rarefaction of molecules, it therefore follows that some sort of a medium is necessary. In the mid-1600s, Robert Boyle noted the absence of sound as he pumped the air out of a jar containing a ringing bell.

Sound travels through air at roughly 330 meters per second (0 degrees C; dry air), significantly slower than light. The speed of sound in other mediums varies according to how close the molecules are known to be. In descending order, sound travels the fastest through solids, then liquids, then gases. Measuring the speed of sound in precise quantities will be difficult for students. Therefore, we must rely upon real-world situations with which they may have had experiences, e.g., lightning and thunder delays; the swing and delay of the crack of a bat at a Major League baseball game, echoes, etc. In general, we want students to realize that sound must have a medium through which to travel, its speed varies according to the mediums, and sound travels significantly slower than light.

A station format is suggested for this lesson since many of the activities are relatively brief, and some require materials that are not easily obtained in sets. It may be useful to enlist the help of a parent/ guardian volunteer. As usual, instructors are invited to adapt the activities to the format that best suits their teaching situation. Enjoy!

Arrange the station-type mini-activities as described below, according to sound traveling through: solids, liquids, and gases.

Sound Travels Through Solids

1. **Strings and Spoons Task Description**

   Tie two 25-cm lengths of string to metal spoons, forks, and table knives. Students should hold the ends of the strings to their ears, one on each side. Gently tap the spoon against a hard surface, such as a desk. Observe the results using the senses of hearing and touch. Repeat with plastic spoons, forks, and knives. Compare and contrast the results.

2. **Table-Top Tapping**

   Working in pairs, have one student stand at the end of a long, wooden, conference-type table. The student should gently tap steadily on the table top with his/her finger or a small wooden mallet. The partner should stand at the other end of the table and listen for the tapping sound. Obviously, he/she will hear the tapping as the sound waves travel through the air to the other end of the table. Next, continue the tapping (steadily, as before) as the student lays his/her head down with his/her ear pressed against the table. The listening student should hold the other ear shut with his/her finger. Compare the sounds and infer

Name: _____ Date: _____

STUDENT INQUIRY ACTIVITY 4 : IN WHAT WAYS DO SOUNDS TRAVEL? (CONT.)

that the sound is louder (travels better) through the table than the air. The listener may toggle back and forth between the air (standing upright) and head on the table, while the other student taps steadily at the same intensity.

Sound Travels Through Liquids

1. Wind a small alarm clock or wristwatch with an audible ticking sound. Encourage students to listen to the ticking sound. In this manner, the sound will travel through the air. Next, seal the clock in an airtight resealable plastic bag. Submerge the sealed bag inside of a gallon-sized bag that contains water. The idea is to try to transmit sound through the water. The student should place his/her ear next to the bag of water and observe using the sense of hearing. Repeat the activity while submerging the clock in a glass tank of water. Compare the results. Take the clock out of the bag and repeat the activity with the clock on the other side of the tank; listen through the tank. See if the students realize that they are also actually hearing the ticking through air with the outer ear. Observe to see if the students realize it is necessary to close the outer ear. Observe to see if the students also recognize that they are actually testing sound as it travels through glass and water, and plastic and water, for that matter.

2. If you are fortunate enough to have access to a swimming pool, encourage students to create sounds while under water, e.g., voices, clapping, snapping, etc. Compare these sounds with those made exactly the same way, only above the surface of the water. Finally, compare this to heads under water and sound made above water.

Sound Travels Through Gases

1. Working in pairs, have students spilt into two groups, sound makers and listeners. Have students report to opposite ends of the football field; sound makers at one end, listeners at the other end. The sound maker group should have sound-making devices such as thump sticks, which are flat boards with handles that can be clapped together. Assign one student to be the signaler; the signaler's role is to signify the exact moment the sound is made. For example, as the thump sticks are whacked together, the signaler could drop his/her arm, thereby signaling the moment the sound was created. The listeners should focus on the signaler, yet listen for the sound.

    An alternative to the student signaler would be to enlist the assistance of the physical education teacher and/or track coach. He/she would likely have access to a starter gun used by track officials to start races. The gun fires blanks, yet emits a small puff of smoke easily observed from a distance.

    Allow students to experiment with greater distances and closer distances. Compare the results and findings. Don't forget to switch groups so all students can experience the delay in sound as it travels through air.

Name: _____ Date: _____

STUDENT INQUIRY ACTIVITY 4 : IN WHAT WAYS DO SOUNDS TRAVEL? (CONT.)

2. Repeat the activity with a strong light. Have the signaler drop his/her arm the minute the beacon is turned on. Have students observe the differences in delay between when the listeners could hear the sounds after they were made; observe the differences between when listeners could see the light after it was turned on.

Procedures:

1. Ask students to predict and record whether or not they believe that sound travels. Require them to provide a rationale; observe for application of previously learned concepts, e.g., waves, vibrations, etc.

2. Ask students to predict the order in which they believe sound travels the fastest (solids, liquids, and gases) and provide a rationale; observe for evidence of real-world experiences, e.g., swimming pool, baseball games, echoes, etc.

3. Discuss student ideas and try to reach class consensus on concepts related to the travel of sounds. Record any questions that arise from the discussion, particularly those that can be investigated using an inquiry approach later on.

4. Explain that since we do not have the technology needed to make precise sound measurements, in some cases, we must rely on another definition of the speed of sound. In some cases, we will listen to which sounds appear to be better according to loudness. Provide a brief overview of essential directions at each station.

5. Following the station activities, encourage students to share their results and conclusions. As before, record questions that arise as a result of any of the activities and/or ensuing discussion.

6. Specifically, ask students to speculate why sounds appear to travel slower in gases than in both solids and liquids. Refer to a sketch of the molecules in the three states of matter. See if students are able to infer why sounds travel slower in gases than in solids and liquids after seeing the diagram. Encourage them to recall what they have learned about vibrations.

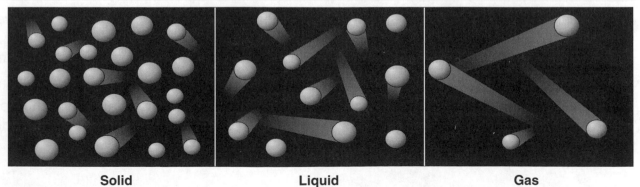

| **Solid** | **Liquid** | **Gas** |

38

Name: _____ Date: _____

STUDENT INQUIRY ACTIVITY **4**: IN WHAT WAYS DO SOUNDS TRAVEL? (CONT.)

Exploration/Data Collection:

Traveling Sounds

1. Using your *Sound Off!* journal, record a response to the following statement. Provide a detailed rationale to your reasoning.

> True or False: Sound travels.

2. Rank in order, with 1 = fastest and 3 = slowest, the types of substances through which sound travels.

_____ liquids   _____ gases   _____ solids

I believe this is true because …

_____

_____

_____

_____

_____

_____

_____

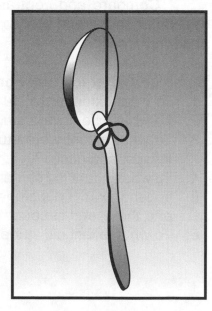

A note to all good students who are interested in the science of sounds—we teachers always appreciate when you make predictions of what will happen before trying each activity. Of course, feel free to read through the directions in order to make a good prediction. Also, after trying the activities and recording your observations, please don't forget to include an explanation of why you think things happened.

Sound Travels Through Solids

Using your *Sound Off!* journal, record any observations you made with the hanging spoons, forks, and knives. Describe what senses you used to make these observations. Record any questions you have and/or note if additional information is needed.

Name: _____ Date: _____

STUDENT INQUIRY ACTIVITY **4** : IN WHAT WAYS DO SOUNDS TRAVEL? (CONT.)

Using your *Sound Off!* journal, record any observations you made with the table-top tapping. Describe what senses you used to make these observations. Record any questions you have and/or note if additional information is needed.

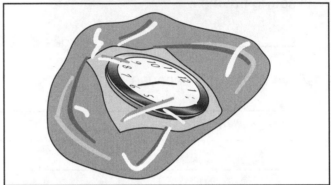

Sound Travels Through Liquids

Using your *Sound Off!* journal, record any observations you made with the clock and water. Describe what senses you used to make these observations. Record any questions you have and/or note if additional information is needed.

Answer this question in your *Sound Off!* journal: Do you think the placement of the clock is important in this activity? Why or why not?

Sound Travels Through Gases

Using your *Sound Off!* journal, record any observations you made with the long-distance sounds. Describe what senses you used to make these observations. Record any questions you have and/or note if additional information is needed.

Compare and contrast the apparent speeds of sound and light, based upon your observations.

Summary/What to Look For:
1. To what extent were students able to explain that sound travels?
2. To what extent were students able to infer that a medium is needed for sound to travel?
3. To what extent were students able to infer that sounds travel differently through solids, liquids, and gases?
4. To what extent did students identify differences in the speed of sound in varying mediums?
5. To what extent did students synthesize the relationship of vibrations, longitudinal waves, and the speed of sound?
6. To what extent did students accurately compare the speed of sound to the speed of light?

40

Name: _____ Date: _____

STUDENT INQUIRY ACTIVITY 4: IN WHAT WAYS DO SOUNDS TRAVEL? (CONT.)

Discussion Questions/Assessment:

1. Using the *Sound Off!* journal, students should record something they learned from the large-group follow-up discussion that they had not previously considered.

2. Strike a tuning fork and hold it next to, but not touching, your ear. Listen to the sound that is made, particularly the intensity. Now, strike a tuning fork and place the base against your head. Compare and explain the difference in your *Sound Off!* journal.

3. Apply your understanding of how sound and light travel by explaining how you can determine the distance (from you) that a lightning bolt strikes.

4. Return to your rank order of sound travel. Using a different color of marking device, alter it, if needed, based upon what you have learned in this lesson.

5. Return to the original essay you wrote about everything you believe to be true about sound. Using a different writing instrument, edit anything you wish to change. Add any new information from these activities about which you feel confident.

6. Encourage students to illustrate their understanding of how sound travels through various mediums on the cover of the *Sound Off!* journals.

Extensions/Real-World Applications:

1. One day, you notice that you see a jet fly over, but don't hear its sound until later. Research the reason for this.

2. Research to find out about the various races held in track meets. Using your knowledge of how sound travels, why do manufacturers include a small puff of smoke on the starter gun?

3. Create a table for the speed of sound in various mediums. Include a comparison to the speed of light.

4. Create a conversion table for the speed of sound, e.g., English Standard to metric. Add formulas that can be used to convert units.

Name: _____ Date: _____

STUDENT INQUIRY ACTIVITY **5** : HOW ARE SOUNDS MEASURED?

Topic: Sound—Measurement

Introductory Statement

One of the most important skills of scientists is measurement. In this lesson, you will discover how scientists measure sounds. You will also learn what levels of sounds are harmful to the human ear.

NSES Content Standard A: Understandings About Scientific Inquiry

Technology is used to gather data, enhances accuracy, and allows scientists to analyze and quantify results of investigations.

Science Skills and Concepts:

- Students will identify the unit of measurement for volume of sound.
- Students will cite ranges of decibels that are acceptable and not acceptable for humans.
- Students will infer types of human activity that may be harmful to humans' ears.

Materials/Safety Concerns:

Sound Off! journal
A sound meter, if available
Reference materials regarding sound, including trade books, encyclopedias, etc.
Internet access

Content Background:

The intensity of sound is measured in **decibels (dB)**. Decibel levels for humans range from 0, the very threshold of human hearing, to 180, a rocket engine. Even though humans may be physically able to hear very loud sounds, it is often at a cost. Human ears can be damaged with prolonged periods of sounds at the 68–75 decibel range. Irreversible damage can begin at roughly 130 decibels.

It is important for students to be able to recognize safe levels of sound and methods to protect their hearing. Therefore, students should become aware of the impact of their daily activities on their health and ability to hear. This lesson will focus on how sound intensity is measured and labeled. Students will assess their daily activities and attempt to measure the sounds therein. You will need to have reference materials available regarding decibel scales and sound safety. Basic sound meters can easily be obtained through most science supply companies, but they can be rather costly. Many sound meters are easily used with either a Macintosh or PC. If budgetary restrictions disallow you to purchase a sound meter, you could perhaps check with the high school physics department for a loaner.

Name: _____ Date: _____

STUDENT INQUIRY ACTIVITY **5** : HOW ARE SOUNDS MEASURED? (CONT.)

Procedures:

1. Ask students to speculate how scientists measure sounds. They may refer to the measurement of speed, frequency, and loudness. Point out that this lesson will focus on how scientists measure the intensity, or loudness, of sound.

2. Ask students to recall any sounds that hurt their ears. Have students explain the context within which these sounds were heard.

3. Ask students to speculate whether or not they believe that human hearing can be damaged irreversibly. Attempt to clarify their beliefs of what types of sounds would cause irreversible damage.

4. Ask students to log 10–12 different sounds/activities per day for two weeks of normal activity. Have them represent a variety of sounds within the context of their daily activities, such as working on homework, playing on the playground, attending a concert, taking a relative to the airport, mowing the lawn, etc.

5. Encourage students to research to find various decibel scales and accompanying descriptions of activities for each decibel level. These may vary slightly. If some of the students' journal entries are not represented on any of the scales, try to choose the most similar activity represented.

6. Have them determine safe levels of sound for the human ear. Assign students to evaluate their sound experiences for the period of time logged. Examine the data for trends, e.g., I'm clearly exposed to louder sounds on the weekend.

   Instruct students to self-assess and give themselves a "sound-safety" grade and accompanying rationale for the grade. If the grade is below a *C*, ask students to include a plan of action to correct the sound situation.

7. As a closure activity, invite an audiologist to speak to the students regarding sound safety. Have students generate questions based upon their sound logs and self-assessment.

Name: _____ Date: _____

STUDENT INQUIRY ACTIVITY **5** : HOW ARE SOUNDS MEASURED? (CONT.)

Exploration/Data Collection:

Turn Down the Volume

1. Record ways in which you believe scientists measure sounds.

    _____

    _____

    _____

    _____

2. Record any sounds that you can recall as having hurt your ears. Describe the context of the setting.

    _____

    _____

    _____

    _____

3. Using your *Sound Off!* journal, create a data collection chart to record 10–12 different sounds/activities you experience daily. Record data for a period of at least two weeks, or longer if you like. Record the context in which the sounds were heard. For example, one entry might look like this: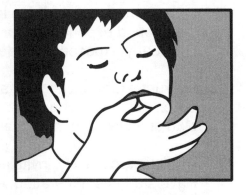

    "I went to a circus where roughly 5,000 people were cheering loudly, and the person next to me whistled shrilly, with two fingers in his mouth. The circus was held indoors."

4. Analyze your sound log for decibel levels. Research to find decibel ranges; use the Internet, trade books, and encyclopedias. Watch for and note trends in your daily sound experiences. Record this in your *Sound Off!* journal.

5. Using your *Sound Off!* journal, examine your data analysis. What conclusions can you draw regarding your sound experiences over the past two weeks, particularly in light of sound safety? As a self-assessment, assign yourself a "sound-safety" grade. Provide a detailed rationale for your grade, as you may need to defend this to your teacher and classmates. If you assigned yourself a grade lower than *C*, consider a plan of action to increase your sound-safety behavior.

Name: _____ Date: _____

STUDENT INQUIRY ACTIVITY **5** : HOW ARE SOUNDS MEASURED? (CONT.)

6. Record in your *Sound Off!* journal activities that you think may be harmful to humans' ears. In what ways can these activities be made safer?

Loud Sounds

1. Jet
2. Race car
3. Horn
4. Scream
5. Headphones
6. Stereo

7. Based on these experiences, record questions you may have for a professional who tests humans' ability to hear. Be prepared to ask those questions, in the event you are fortunate enough to have a guest speaker.

Summary/What to Look For:
1. To what extent were students able to identify the unit of measurement for volume of sound?
2. To what extent were students able to cite ranges of decibels that are acceptable and not acceptable for themselves?
3. To what extent were students able to infer types of human activity that may be harmful to humans' ears?
4. To what extent were students able to analyze and evaluate their sound experiences?

Discussion Questions/Assessment:
1. Essay: Based upon what you have learned about measuring sound and its effects on humans' ears, describe various careers that could be completed within the safe range of decibels. Describe some careers that are not in the safe range; what might these people do to protect their hearing?

2. Return to the original essay you wrote about everything you believe to be true about sound. Using a different writing instrument, edit anything you wish to change. Add any new information from these activities about which you feel confident.

3. Encourage students to illustrate their understanding of how sound intensity is measured on the cover of the *Sound Off!* journals.

Extensions/Real-World Applications:
1. Another way to "see" sound is via a technological instrument known as an oscilloscope. Research to find out more about oscilloscopes and their functions.

2. Some health professionals rely upon sound in the form of sonograms. What are sonograms and how do they relate to the measurement of sound? What career options are related to sonograms?

3. Decipher the relationship between the decibel and a famous inventor named Alexander Graham Bell.

Name: _____ Date: _____

STUDENT INQUIRY ACTIVITY **6** : ECHOES ... ECHOES ... ECHOES ...

Topic: Sound—Echoes

Introductory Statement:

     We have learned that sound travels at varying speeds, depending upon the medium through which it passes. In this lesson, you will discover what happens when sounds encounter substances through which they can't pass.

NSES Content Standard B: Transfer of Energy

Energy is a property of many substances and is associated with heat, light, electricity, mechanical motion, sound, nuclei, and the nature of a chemical. Energy is transferred in many ways.

NSES Content Standard A: Abilities Necessary to Do Scientific Inquiry
- Identify questions that can be answered through scientific investigations
- Design and conduct a scientific investigation
- Use appropriate tools and techniques to gather, analyze, and interpret data
- Develop descriptions, explanations, predictions, and models using evidence
- Think critically and logically to make the relationships between evidence and explanations
- Recognize and analyze alternative explanations and predictions
- Communicate scientific procedures and explanations
- Use mathematics in all aspects of scientific inquiry

Scientific Skills and Concepts:
- Students will define an echo as a reflection of sound waves.
- Students will infer that various surface types affect what happens to sound waves.
- Students will analyze the relationship between time and distance within the context of echoes.
- Students will identify geophysical features of the earth that naturally lend themselves to echoes.

Materials/Safety Concerns:

Sound Off! journals

Thump sticks or other loud, sound-making devices that are easily repeatable

Large expanse of brick wall or similar surface, e.g., the side of a gymnasium

Stopwatch or timing device with tenths of seconds

Internet access

Materials as needed, pending students' requests

Geophysical reference materials

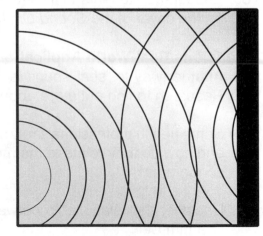

Name: _____   Date: _____

STUDENT INQUIRY ACTIVITY **6**: ECHOES … ECHOES … ECHOES … (CONT.)

Content Background:

Echoes are reflections of sound waves when they encounter a hard surface through which they cannot pass and/or are not absorbed. Echoes are directly proportional to the distance between the original source and the reflecting surface. As the distance increases, so does the time it takes for the echo to return. As students have previously learned, sound energy travels in longitudinal waves. Unimpeded, sounds fade as they get farther and farther away from the original source. If students are too far away from the original sound, and depending on the original intensity, they may never even hear the sound. For example, students may visually observe a jet flying high overhead but be unable to hear the roar of the engines. Sound waves react differently when they strike various surfaces. This is especially dependent upon the texture of the surface. For instance, if the surface struck by the sound is soft and porous, a portion of the sound will likely become absorbed. Whereas, if the surface struck by the sound is relatively hard and flat, the sound waves are likely to bounce off, or be reflected. This provides the context in which to study echoes.

Understanding the reflection of sound waves is best suited within the context of the real world. Therefore, this lesson is designed to present the physical science of echoes and increase students' awareness of the geophysical features on Earth that are likely to produce echoes. Ideally, it would be great to study echoes in a large canyon or a cave. More pragmatically, most elementary and middle schools have a large exterior wall, e.g., the side of a gymnasium is effective for reflecting sounds. It is best if the wall is somewhat sheltered and surrounded by concrete or asphalt. Instructors may wish to vary the activities according to the learning environment.

Procedures:

1. Return to the list of sounds students made in the previous lessons. Ask a volunteer to repeat one of his/her sounds. Ask students to describe the sound and, most importantly, tell what happened to the sound, e.g., Where did it go?

2. Ask for a volunteer to share a sound that clearly fades out slowly, e.g., a triangle ringing after being struck. Ask students to compare that sound to one that ends more abruptly, e.g., clapping your hands one time.

3. Ask the students to recall what they have learned about the nature of sound waves and how they travel. Have students re-read what they have just written and explained. Provide them with an opportunity to enhance their journal entries. Encourage them to share any improvements with the class.

Name: _____ Date: _____

STUDENT INQUIRY ACTIVITY 6: ECHOES ... ECHOES ... ECHOES ... (CONT.)

4. Ask students to define what they believe to be an echo; encourage them to use sketches and diagrams, if necessary. Ask students if any of the sounds so far were a result of an echo. Discuss their responses. Introduce echoes in relation to the idea of reflection. Ask students to think of what factors may be necessary to create an echo. List their ideas on the chalkboard or on chart paper.

5. Ask students for ideas on how to create echoes of their own. Offer them the ability to work outside and allow them to request materials as needed. Allow students to plan and conduct the making of echoes. Have students record their plans and observations in the *Sound Off!* journals.

6. Briefly regroup and discuss the results. Provide a challenge: "Using your echo-making devices, demonstrate a relationship between time and distance." Have students create a hypothesis regarding time and distance within the context of sound. Encourage them to identify variables that need to be controlled, provide operational definitions, and list step-by-step procedures, all prior to beginning.

7. After students collect data, encourage them to analyze the data and draw conclusions. Encourage students to use sketches and diagrams in their analyses. Have them prepare a laboratory report suitable for presentation to their classmates; create the lab report on blank overhead transparencies. Students should be reminded of the importance of speaking and listening skills during the presentations. The audience should act in the role of critics regarding the inquiry process.

8. Conclude the discussion of echoes with an assignment to find the best place in the world for echoes (geophysical features in nature). Have students research to find and defend their choices. Take a class poll for the most popular geophysical features. Discuss the merits/demerits of the various locations. Require students to apply their knowledge of echoes and sound waves as they make and defend their choices.

9. Return to the original journal entries from steps 1–3 above. Offer students the opportunity to edit as they wish.

Name: _____ Date: _____

STUDENT INQUIRY ACTIVITY 6 : ECHOES … ECHOES … ECHOES … (CONT.)

Exploration/Data Collection:

Echoes … Echoes … Echoes …

1. Listen to a sound made by one of your classmates, as directed by your instructor. Using your *Sound Off!* journal, describe the sound and tell what eventually happens to it.

2. Pretend that you have just been approached by a friend who has never heard of the word *echo* and has absolutely no idea what it is. In your *Sound Off!* journal, define what you believe to be an echo. Use sketches and diagrams if necessary.

3. Design a plan to create echoes. Create a list of materials you will need as well as a step-by-step description of your intent. Be sure to have your plan approved by the instructor before beginning.

4. Echo … Echo … Echo … Challenge … Challenge … Challenge …

    Challenge: What is the relationship between the time and distance of a manmade echo?

Carefully read and think about the challenge listed above. If and when you choose to accept the challenge, sign the acceptance form and prepare to begin planning.

I hereby accept the challenge:

_____
              signed   date

Using your *Sound Off!* journal, be sure to include information for each of the major headings listed below:
*   Research Question
*   Research Hypothesis
*   Materials Needed
*   Operational Definitions
*   Variables to Control
*   Procedures
*   Analysis
*   Conclusions

5. Prepare a lab report suitable for presentation to your classmates. Be prepared to answer any questions they may have. For convenience, you may wish to transfer your information onto a blank overhead transparency. Good luck!! … Good luck!! … Good luck!!

STUDENT INQUIRY ACTIVITY **6**: ECHOES ... ECHOES ... ECHOES ... (CONT.)

6. Research and locate the very best natural, geophysical feature in the world for making and listening to echoes. Using your *Sound Off!* journal, prepare a rationale for why you chose this feature. Map the feature and be prepared to defend your choice in a large-group discussion.

7. In your *Sound Off!* journal, record any questions you may have regarding echoes and the reflection of sound. You will have a chance to consider investigating these questions during a later lesson.

Summary/What to Look For:
1. To what extent did students accurately define an echo as a reflection of sound waves?
2. To what extent did students accurately infer that various surface types affect what happens to sound waves?
3. To what extent did students accurately analyze the relationship between time and distance within the context of echoes?
4. To what extent did students accurately identify geophysical features of the earth which naturally lend themselves to echoes?

Discussion Questions/Assessment:

1. A large bell is rung one time. Describe where the sound goes, what happens to it, and why.

_____

_____

_____

_____

_____

2. What factors influence whether or not there will be an echo?

_____

_____

_____

_____

STUDENT INQUIRY ACTIVITY 6: ECHOES … ECHOES … ECHOES … (CONT.)

3. Describe the relationship between time and distance when considering echoes.

    _____

    _____

    _____

    _____

    _____

4. Return to the original essay you wrote about everything you believe to be true about sound. Using a different writing instrument, edit anything you wish to change. Add any new information from these activities in which you feel confident.

5. Encourage students to illustrate their understanding of echoes on the cover of the *Sound Off!* journals.

Extension/Real-World Applications:

1. Cooperate with the music teacher on the research/study of the science of acoustics. Pretend that you are hired to provide interior design for a new music hall. Based upon what you know about echoes and music, what types of decisions would be part of your planning?

Name: _____ Date: _____

STUDENT INQUIRY ACTIVITY 7 : SOUNDS IN NATURE

Topic: Sound—Animal Adaptations

Introductory Statement:

Sound plays an important role in animal communication, self-defense, and navigation purposes. In this lesson, you will discover and investigate special adaptations in some animals that rely heavily on sound for their survival.

NSES Content Standard C: Structure and Function in Living Systems
Living systems at all levels of organization demonstrate the complementary nature of structure and function.

NSES Content Standard C: Regulation and Behavior
Behavior is one kind of response an organism can make to an internal or environmental stimulus. A behavioral response requires coordination and communication at many levels, including cells, organ systems, and whole organisms.

Science Skills and Concepts:
- Students will identify animals that rely on sound for navigational purposes.
- Students will identify animals that rely on sound for self-defense.
- Students will identify sounds that animals use to communicate.
- Students will infer the importance of sounds in ecology.

Materials/Safety Concerns:
Sound Off! journal
Reference materials regarding food chains and ecology
Field guides to mammals, amphibians, reptiles, birds, fish
Internet access

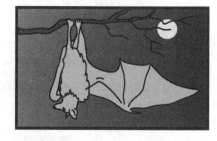

Content Background:

Many animals rely on sounds and their ability to sense sounds in order to communicate, defend themselves, and locate food. In this lesson, students will be asked to identify an animal of choice and investigate its adaptations regarding sounds. This is a good opportunity to differentiate between ultrasonic sound and infrasonic adaptations. **Ultrasonic sounds** are well above the human range of hearing, yet animals such as microbats (small bats) rely heavily upon a process called **echolocation** both to navigate and to locate food. Microbats emit a series of high-pitched sounds that echo, or bounce off, objects, thereby providing information regarding the location of the object. As the microbat nears the object, increased sounds are emitted and reflected, which in turn provide increased information. Shrews and dolphins are examples of other mammals that rely upon echolocation. **Infrasonic sounds** are slightly below the human range of hearing. Large animals, such as elephants and sea mammals, emit these sounds. These sounds can travel many miles, and they serve as a communicative device for grouping. Other animals with sounds of interest may include sea lions barking, sperm whales clicking, walruses whistling, and humpback whales' music. Finally, many animals create sounds

Name: _____ Date: _____

STUDENT INQUIRY ACTIVITY 7: SOUNDS IN NATURE (CONT.)

to communicate danger. Rabbits may shriek when endangered; beavers may slap the water with their tails if danger is perceived. In any case, students should identify the physical characteristics that are adapted to sending and receiving sounds. Three excellent trade books for reference use include *Whales* by Vassili Papastavrou, *The Five Senses of the Animal World: Hearing* by Andreu Llamas, and *Animals: How They Work* by David Burne. Please see the reference list at the back of this book for complete bibliographic information.

Procedures:

1. In order to set the context of the lesson, ask students to record ways in which animals rely upon sound. Encourage them to be specific by naming animals and how they depend upon sounds. Lead a large-group discussion about why sounds are important to animals. List students' ideas on the chalkboard or chart paper. Attempt to classify the ideas and generate main categories.

2. Have students choose a specific animal and category for research. Have students generate a list of specific questions for their animal or category of choice. An example may include:

   Animal/Category – Bats and Echolocation
   Questions of Interest to Me ...
   a. What is echolocation, and how does it work?
   b. Do all bats rely upon echolocation? If not, how do others navigate?
   c. Do bats have ears? If not, what do they use to hear sounds?
   d. How do bats use echolocation in open areas where there is nothing off of which the sound waves can bounce?
   e. To what extent do bats rely on their eyes for navigation?
   f. How does echolocation help bats to find and capture food?

   Note: students may need help refining their lists of questions. Perhaps use peer and/or teacher edit prior to launching the investigations.

3. As before, point out the importance of students writing a procedure/plan to investigate their questions. Remind students to make efforts to apply previously learned sound content and have them record the plans in their *Sound Off!* journals.

4. Provide assistance with locating needed resources and materials to investigate the questions generated by students.

5. Encourage students to share their results and findings regarding the questions under investigation. As before, stress the importance of excellent speaking and listening skills. Encourage the audience to ask good questions of the presenters. Point out the cyclical nature of science, e.g., good inquiry generates new questions for additional inquiry.

6. Encourage students to display their findings.

Name: _____ Date: _____

STUDENT INQUIRY ACTIVITY **7** : SOUNDS IN NATURE (CONT.)

Exploration/Data Collection:

Animals and Sound

1. Using your *Sound Off!* journal, brainstorm a list of animals that rely on sound for survival. Be sure to include specifically the manner in which the animals use sound. Be prepared to share your thoughts with others.

2. From the class list, select an animal that most interests you. This is the animal you can research regarding its use of sound. You may choose an animal you know little or nothing about, or you may choose an animal with which you are familiar but would like to know more. In your *Sound Off!* journal, list the animal and generate a list of questions of interest to you. Specifically, generate questions about the animal and sound. These may include questions about how animals use sound to defend themselves, how animals use sound to locate food, how animals communicate, how animals hear, adaptations of animals that help them to hear, etc.

3. Next, list possible resources needed to investigate your questions. Do not limit yourself to simply one or two sources of information. Be thorough in your investigation!

4. Finally, carefully design a plan of action. For example, how do you plan to use the resources to answer your questions? How will you organize the findings? What will happen if you are unable to answer some of the questions? How will you handle new questions that arise as a result of your investigation? How will you share your findings with others?

    Be sure to have your plan approved by the instructor prior to beginning. Good luck!

5. Complete the investigation according to your plan. Discuss how you will share your findings with others and with your instructor.

Summary/What to Look For:
1. To what extent were students able to identify animals that rely on sound for navigational purposes?
2. To what extent were students able to identify animals that rely on sound for self-defense?
3. To what extent were students able to identify sounds that animals use to communicate?
4. To what extent were students able to infer the importance of sounds in ecology?
5. To what extent were students able to accurately communicate their findings with others?
6. To what extent did students utilize effective listening and speaking skills?

Name: _____ Date: _____

STUDENT INQUIRY ACTIVITY 7: SOUNDS IN NATURE (CONT.)

Discussion Questions/Assessment:

1. List several examples of animals that use echolocation to find food.

   _____

   _____

   _____

   _____

2. List several examples of animals that use sounds to communicate.

   _____

   _____

   _____

   _____

3. List several examples of animals that use sounds to defend themselves and/or their young.

   _____

   _____

   _____

   _____

4. List several animals with unique physical characteristics that enable them to send and/or receive sounds.

   _____

   _____

   _____

   _____

Name: _____ Date: _____

STUDENT INQUIRY ACTIVITY 7 : SOUNDS IN NATURE (CONT.)

5. Return to the original essay you wrote about everything you believe to be true about sound. Using a different writing instrument, edit anything you wish to change. Add any new information from these activities about which you feel confident.

6. Encourage students to illustrate how animals are dependent upon sound for survival and communication on the cover of the *Sound Off!* journals.

Extension/Real-World Applications:

1. As a closure activity, conduct a game of animal charades. Students should act out the animals, particularly the sound-related adaptations the animals use for communication and survival.

2. Challenge students to draw parallels between animals' use of echolocation and humans' use of sonar.

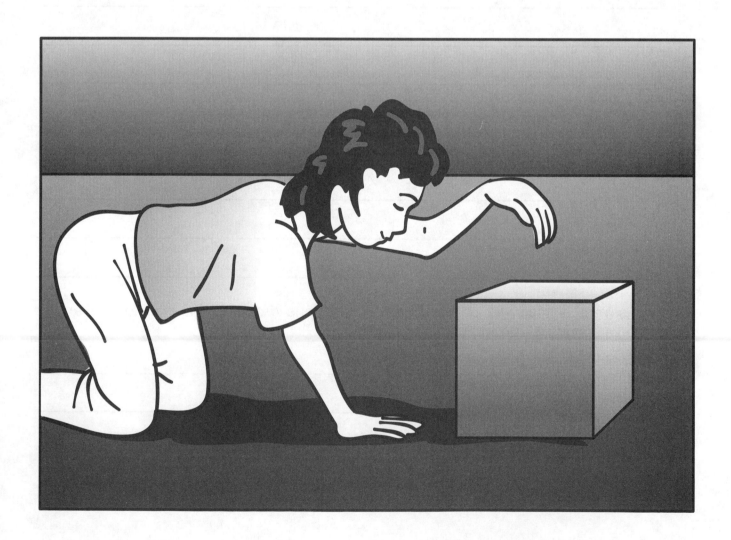

Name: _____ Date: _____

STUDENT INQUIRY ACTIVITY 8 : EARS TO YOU!

Topic: Sound—The Human Ear

Introductory Statement:
Earlier, you discovered the importance of sounds to animals. In this lesson, you will learn about the role of the human ear in hearing sounds.

NSES Content Standard C: Structure and Function in Living Systems
Living systems at all levels of organization demonstrate the complementary nature of structure and function.

NSES Content Standard C: Regulation and Behavior
Behavior is one kind of response an organism can make to an internal or environmental stimulus. A behavioral response requires coordination and communication at many levels, including cells, organ systems, and whole organisms.

Science Skills and Concepts:
- Students will identify the parts and functions of the human ear.
- Students will infer how mechanical energy is converted into messages that are sent to the human brain.

Materials/Safety Concerns:
Access to cross-sectional diagrams of the human ear or a large model of the human ear
Age-appropriate trade books and reference materials related to sound and the sense of hearing
Internet access
Construction paper
Masking tape
Glue
Scissors
Markers
Chart paper
Shoeboxes and cardboard
Tagboard
Fine-mesh screen
Papier-mâché supplies (flour, water, newspaper strips)
String

Content Background:
The human ear has three main sections: 1) *the outer ear*, which collects the sounds and directs them into the middle ear; 2) *the middle ear*, which contains the **hammer**, **anvil**, and **stirrup**, all small bones that increase the size of sound vibrations; and 3) *the inner ear*, where vibrations are converted to electrical signals and are sent to the brain for interpretation. The outer ear is sometimes called the **pinna** or **auricle**. The bones found in the middle ear are among the smallest bones in the body, yet serve the purpose of amplifying the incoming sound

STUDENT INQUIRY ACTIVITY 8: EARS TO YOU! (CONT.)

waves. Inside the liquid-filled **cochlea**, tiny hair cells are moved, causing the stimulation of nerves, which are in turn detected by the brain via the nervous system.

Models are critical in elementary and middle-school science. Models provide elementary and middle-level science students with exposure and access to areas and phenomena that they would not normally be able to experience. Building and utilizing models is considered one of the important process skills in the inquiry process. However, creating models can require extensive time and some unique materials. Each instructor should weigh the benefits of models as he/she considers the utility of student-generated models.

In this lesson, students are asked to research the parts of the human ear/hearing process and build models that reflect the form and function of each part. Ideally, each model part created by students should fit together to form a complete ear. If this is to be the case, the model parts will need to be built as closely to scale as possible. Students should work in small groups, depending upon class size and available materials. Additional parts for student research include the ear canal, cochlear nerve, brain, electrical impulses, Eustachian tube, stapes, and eardrum. An acceptable alternative to building models might include cross-sectional diagrams with accompanying labels and captions describing the function of each part. Finally, you could perhaps check with the high school biology department for an existing model of the human ear.

Procedures:

1. In their *Sound Off!* journals, ask students to record what they believe happens as humans hear a sound, e.g., the hearing process. Urge them to describe carefully how the sound is sensed and understood. Do not give them too much guidance at this point, since your main goal is to discover their perceptions of how humans hear sounds. Put this information aside for later use in the lesson.

2. Explain the role of models in science; especially in cases where the phenomena is not overtly observable. Challenge the class with the task of creating a large, cross-sectional model of the human ear.

3. In order to meet the challenge, students must research to determine each of the crucial parts of the ear (see content background information) and their roles in hearing. Students should prepare a list of 8–10 parts of the ear/hearing apparatus. As data is collected, record it on chart paper, and discuss which parts should be represented on the model.

4. As a class, decide the format of the model. Three-dimensional models are effective and can be made using papier-mâché, cardboard, Styrofoam™, fine-mesh screen, wire, etc. One suggestion is to secure the advice/guidance of the resident art teacher if a three-dimensional model is selected. The three-dimensional model provides an opportunity to consider scale, so that the individual parts to be manufactured by the students all fit together.

   Note: If the materials needed to build a three-dimensional model are unavailable, students may wish to create a two-dimensional model on a mural or a large piece of chart paper. Individual models may be constructed in lieu of a class model.

Name: _____ Date: _____

STUDENT INQUIRY ACTIVITY 8 : EARS TO YOU! (CONT.)

5. Next, decide on the way in which students will be grouped and ear/hearing parts are to be assigned.

6. Students should become more familiar with the part for which they are responsible. Students will not only need to manufacture the part, they must also generate an explanation of the function of the part and its importance to the ear/hearing apparatus. This will require further research. In addition, they should consider ways in which they might build the part for the class ear model(s).

7. Assist students as they research and construct the individual parts, as needed. While aesthetics may be sacrificed, maintain a focus on the form and function of the parts as the model(s) is/are constructed.

8. Label each part and attach or display the written explanation of the part and its importance. This may be done on a poster in front of the model(s). Encourage students to read each other's work and ask questions of each other. Since students specialized on one part of the ear/hearing apparatus, they will better understand the entire model by observing and reading the work of others. You may wish to have a formal presentation wherein each group presents its work on the model(s).

9. As closure, ask students to record (again) what they believe happens as humans hear a sound. This response should be recorded in their *Sound Off!* journals as well.

10. Display the model(s) in a location where others in the school can appreciate it.

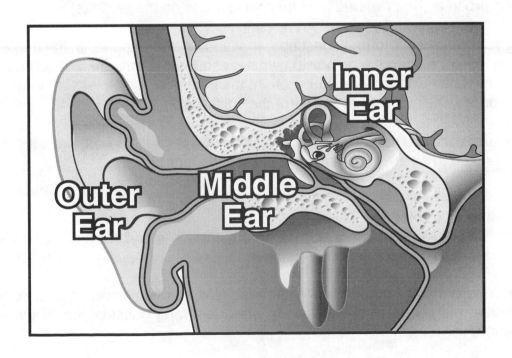

Name: _____ Date: _____

STUDENT INQUIRY ACTIVITY 8 : EARS TO YOU! (CONT.)

Exploration/Data Collection:

Ears to You!

1. Using your *Sound Off!* journal, describe what you believe happens in the human ear when a person hears a sound, e.g., how do we hear sounds?

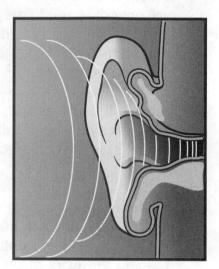

2. In your *Sound Off!* journal, record what you believe to be the major parts of the human ear and hearing process. You will need to apply your research skills to complete this step. Place a star by one or two about which you would like to know more.

3. In your *Sound Off!* journal, record additional information about the part(s) you will construct and contribute to the model of the ear. Specify the function of the part and why it is important in the hearing process.

4. Begin sketching plans about how you might construct this part for the model of the ear. Include the materials you will need and how your part will be fastened to the model(s). Remember, some trial-and-error learning might be necessary.

5. Prepare a label and written explanation of your part; include its role and importance in the hearing process. Be prepared to submit this for use on the model(s).

6. Using your *Sound Off!* journal, describe what you believe happens in the human ear when a person hears a sound, e.g., how do we hear sounds? Compare and contrast your most recent response with the one you wrote at the beginning of the lesson. In what ways are the responses alike? In what ways are they different?

7. Summarize what you have learned about the human ear and the hearing process, especially as they relate to what you already knew about sounds.

Summary/What to Look For:

1. To what extent were students able to identify the parts and functions of the human ear following construction of the ear/hearing model(s)?

2. To what extent were students able to infer how mechanical energy is converted into messages that are sent to the human brain following construction of the ear/hearing model(s)?

STUDENT INQUIRY ACTIVITY **8**: EARS TO YOU! (CONT.)

Discussion Questions/Assessment:

1. Compare and contrast your pre/post responses to what you believe happens in the human ear when a person hears a sound. In what ways are your responses alike? Different? Explain any changes you may observe in the responses.

   _____

   _____

   _____

   _____

2. Summarize what you have learned about the human ear and the hearing process, especially as it relates to what you already knew about sounds.

   _____

   _____

   _____

   _____

3. What questions do you have regarding the human ear and the hearing process, especially as they relate to sounds?

   _____

   _____

   _____

4. Write an essay in which you are a sound that travels through the human ear and into the brain. Detail the steps that occur, along with each of the major parts of the hearing process. Feel free to illustrate the essay if you wish!

5. Return to the original essay you wrote about everything you believe to be true about sound. Using a different writing instrument, edit anything you wish to change. Add any new information from these activities about which you feel confident.

6. Encourage students to illustrate the role of human ears in hearing on the cover of the *Sound Off!* journals.

Name: _____ Date: _____

STUDENT INQUIRY ACTIVITY 8 : EARS TO YOU! (CONT.)

Extensions/Real-World Applications:

1. Present the students with the statement: "True or False: Humans are able to hear all sounds." Have students record their responses and supporting rationale. Compare responses and discuss factors that determine humans' ability to hear, especially as compared to the animals from the previous lesson. Encourage them to share their reasoning. During this discussion, watch for any naive conceptions they may hold.

2. Encourage students to consider people who are deaf or hard of hearing. Using the model of the ear, investigate common causes for this.

3. Investigate technological devices that allow people to overcome deafness and/or hearing deficiencies, e.g., hearing aids, cochlear implants, etc.

4. Identify the relationships between the ear and balance. Involve the physical education teacher in the process.

5. As a small child, you may have had tubes put in your ears. Research to find the nature of these tubes and why they were inserted. What function did they serve? Where did they eventually go?

6. Why is it sometimes difficult to tell where a sound is coming from? For example, have you ever heard a cricket in the room but were unable to locate it?

7. Compare and contrast the human ear to various animals as selected by students.

Name: _____ Date: _____

STUDENT INQUIRY ACTIVITY **9** : HOW DOES THIS CAREER SOUND?

Topic: Sound—Technology

Introductory Statement:
In this lesson, you will consider the importance of sound in our world. Specifically, you will examine the role of sound in various career choices. In addition, you will identify many technology applications related to sound.

Standards for Technological Literacy (STL) – Design
Students will develop an understanding of attributes of design; engineering design; role of troubleshooting, research and development, invention and innovation, and experimentation in problem solving.

Standards for Technological Literacy (STL) – The Designed World
Students will develop an understanding of information and communication technologies.

Standards for Technological Literacy (STL) – The Nature of Technology
Students will develop an understanding of characteristics and scope of technology, core concepts of technology, relationships among technologies, and the connections between technology and other fields of study.

Science Skills and Concepts:
- Students will evaluate the importance of sound in careers of choice.
- Students will infer the importance of technology applications related to sound.

Materials/Safety Concerns:
Internet access
Career reference materials and resources

Content Background:
A broader definition of technology may include anything that helps us to do a job. Using this definition, students should be inclined to consider various careers and the associated sound-related implications. In some cases, sound safety is a major concern, e.g., heavy-equipment operators and other users of loud machinery. In other careers, the quality of sounds is an important component, e.g., audiovisual equipment technicians and musicians. Communication careers depend heavily upon sound and the transfer of information, e.g., air traffic controller and media positions. Finally, many careers involve the restoration of sounds for those with disabilities, e.g., audiologists and medical personnel. These are only a few selected examples of careers that have sound implications. Your students will likely be able to identify others.

63

Name: _____ Date: _____

STUDENT INQUIRY ACTIVITY 9 : HOW DOES THIS CAREER SOUND? (CONT.)

In each of these careers, sound-related technological devices are utilized. The purpose of this lesson is twofold: 1) for students to identify a possible career choice; 2) for students to consider how sounds impact this career, specifically, any technology applications designed specifically to interact with sounds.

Note: The guidance department may serve as an excellent source for career-related materials and resources.

Procedures:

1. Ask students to individually list their top 4–5 career choices at this point in their lives.

2. List the students' choices on the chalkboard or chart paper. As a class, discuss any sound-related implications they may be able to offer. Provide some examples, per content background information.

3. Based upon this discussion, ask students to select a career from their list with distinct sound implications. Students who have less viable sound-related careers may need to reselect according to the criteria of the assignment.

3. Encourage students to generate a list of interview questions for a person who is currently acting in that capacity. Questions should include information about the career itself, sound implications, and any technological devices related to sound.

4. As resources allow, encourage students to contact a person who is currently acting in the career of choice. Live interviews, friendly letters, telephone calls, or e-mail messages are possible forms of communication. If possible, try to utilize local resources, although this may not always be possible. Students will likely have some interest in celebrities, who may not be readily accessible. Adapt the assignment to include these career interests as well. It is highly recommended to incorporate parental involvement in this process. Students should submit their list of questions and interests prior to contacting anyone outside of the school setting.

5. As resources allow, perhaps invite a guest speaker(s) from the community who is actively involved in one of the sound-related careers. Encourage him or her to bring and demonstrate any technology used in the career, e.g., a local telephone technician, a musician trained to use a synthesizer, an audiologist, a doctor, etc.

6. This process may take a period of time. As students garner responses, provide a forum for them to share their findings with others.

7. As closure, ask students to record new questions that have arisen as a result of the responses from the interviews. Allow them to further investigate the career and technology applications using the Internet and other reference materials.

Name: _____ Date: _____

STUDENT INQUIRY ACTIVITY 9: HOW DOES THIS CAREER SOUND? (CONT.)

Exploration/Data Collection:

How Does This Career Sound?

1. Using your *Sound Off!* journal, list the top 4–5 careers you could realistically see yourself being interested in doing after you leave high school and/or college. Briefly explain why you are interested in each of these careers. Be prepared to share your list with others.

2. Following your class discussion, select a career of interest with sound-related implications. Generate a list of questions you have about the career and the impact of sound on this career. Write the questions as you would in an interview format. Be sure to have your list of questions approved by your instructor. Perhaps share your questions with a classmate and seek additional ideas from him/her. In return, help another classmate.

3. With the help and approval of your instructor, attempt to carry out your interview in the form of a friendly letter, e-mail message, telephone call, or live interview. Be sure to secure the permission of your parents before contacting anyone outside the school.

4. If for some reason you are not able to actually ask anyone your questions, conduct on-line research in an attempt to locate the answers. Perhaps your guidance department would be a helpful resource. You may also benefit from talking with other students who have chosen similar careers. Remember, don't forget to focus on sound-related technology within that specific career.

5. As instructed, be ready to share your findings with others.

6. In your *Sound Off!* journal, record a list of new questions that have arisen as a result of your interview and/or research into this career. Specifically, think of questions about sound-related technology in this career.

Name: _____ Date: _____

STUDENT INQUIRY ACTIVITY 9: HOW DOES THIS CAREER SOUND? (CONT.)

Summary/What to Look For:

1. To what extent were students able to evaluate the importance of sound in careers of choice following the research/interviews?
2. To what extent did students infer the importance of technology applications related to sound following the research/interviews?
3. To what extent were students able to generate new questions based on the research/interviews (cyclical nature of inquiry)?

Discussion Questions/Assessment:

1. In what ways has your outlook/attitude toward this career been affected as a result of this experience?

   _____

   _____

   _____

   _____

   _____

   _____

   _____

2. List any new technology you discovered that you previously had not known about.

   _____

   _____

   _____

   _____

   _____

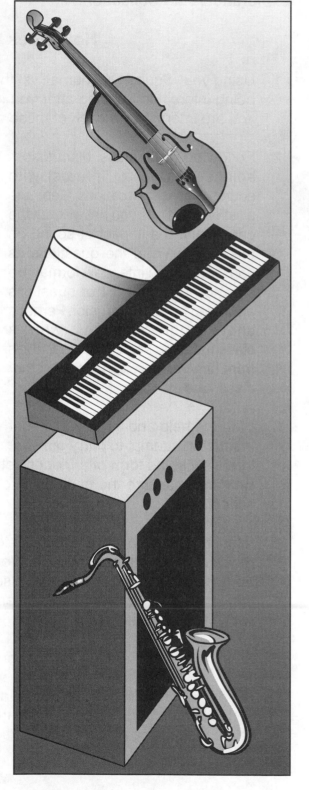

Name: _____ Date: _____

STUDENT INQUIRY ACTIVITY 9: HOW DOES THIS CAREER SOUND? (CONT.)

3. What is the relationship between this career and sounds?

_____

_____

_____

_____

_____

_____

Extensions/Real-World Applications:

1. Return to the concepts learned about sound and the human ear. Investigate technology applications that help those who are deaf or hard of hearing.

2. Research to determine what OSHA stands for. In what ways might OSHA be interested in sounds?

3. In what ways might an architect be interested in sounds as he/she designs buildings, especially music halls?

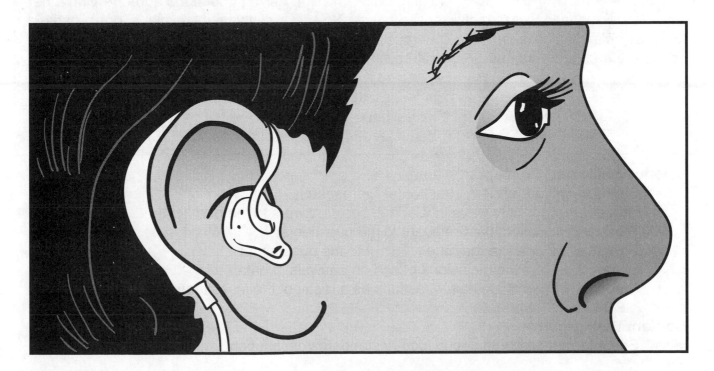

Name: _____ Date: _____

STUDENT INQUIRY ACTIVITY **10** : INDEPENDENT INVESTIGATION

Topic: Sound—Student Inquiry

Introductory Statement:
In this activity, you will identify a question you have about sound, create a plan to answer the question, find the answer(s) to your question, report your findings to others, draw conclusions based on the answer(s) to your question, and identify new questions that emerged as you looked for the answer(s) to the question.

NSES Content Standard A: Understandings About Scientific Inquiry

"Different kinds of questions suggest different kinds of scientific investigations. Some investigations involve observing and describing objects, organisms, or events; some involve collecting specimens; some involve experiments; some involve seeking more information; some involve discovery of new objects and phenomena; and some involve making models.

Current scientific knowledge and understanding guide scientific investigations. Different scientific domains employ different methods, core theories, and standards to advance scientific knowledge and understanding.

Technology is used to gather data accurately and allows scientists to analyze and quantify results of investigations.

Scientific explanations emphasize evidence, have logically consistent arguments, and use scientific principles, models, and theories. The scientific community accepts and uses such explanations until displaced by better scientific ones. When such displacement occurs, science advances.

Science advances through legitimate skepticism. Asking questions and querying other scientists' explanations is part of scientific inquiry. Scientists evaluate the explanations proposed by other scientists by examining evidence, comparing evidence, identifying faulty reasoning, pointing out statements that go beyond evidence, and suggesting alternative explanations for the same observations.

Scientific investigations sometimes result in new ideas and phenomena for study, generate new methods or procedures for an investigation, or develop new technologies to improve the collection of data. All of these results can lead to new investigations." (p. 118)

Science Skills and Concepts:
- Students will generate a question(s) for research.
- Students will identify ways in which to seek answers to the question(s).
- Students will collect data relevant to the question(s).
- Students will analyze the data relevant to the question(s).
- Students will draw conclusions based on analysis of data.
- Students will generate new questions as a result of the investigation.

Content Background:
See information contained in inquiry standards description.

Name: _____ Date: _____

STUDENT INQUIRY ACTIVITY 10 : INDEPENDENT INVESTIGATION (CONT.)

Procedures:

1. Review and explain what it means to approach science from an inquiry point of view. Alert students that in this activity they will have the choice of what to investigate and how to investigate it. Encourage students to review existing questions (from *Sound Off!* journals) or generate questions* they have about sound, perhaps as a result of one or more of the activities previously completed. Assist them with narrowing the focus of the question(s); help them with determining questions that are manageable with available resources. Depending upon the scope and depth of the question(s), students may work individually, in pairs, or in small groups. Require students to develop a "plan of study" to be approved by the teacher.

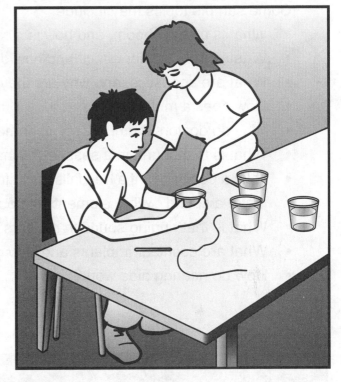

2. As students consider questions of interest, encourage them to consider the following issues:
   - In what ways could I/we find the answer(s)?
   - What types of resources are needed to proceed with the study?
   - Is it possible to design an experiment and collect data?

3. Facilitate student investigations by providing guidance as needed. As the investigations unfold, it may become necessary to help students to reshape the questions; however, encourage students to maintain a focus on what it is they want to know. Guide students as data is collected; check for validity and reliability. Help students with ideas to locate needed resources to conduct investigations.

4. Assist students with formatting the data collected to enhance analysis. Suggest a guiding question such as "What does this data mean?" The key is to interpret the data so conclusions can be drawn. Students should carefully consider how to present the data, along with conclusions drawn and questions for further research.

5. Share the investigations with others. Suggested formats may include: a mini-science conference, a science fair, displays, in-class presentations, etc.

Name: _____ Date: _____

Student Inquiry Activity 10 : Independent Investigation (Cont.)

*   Some sample topics may include:
- What is a sonic boom, and how is it caused?
- What is the Doppler effect, and how does it apply to NASCAR?
- What are acoustics, and why are they important in architecture?
- How does a muffler work?
- Why do doctors thump on my abdomen during a physical and/or check-up?
- What is that sound in a seashell? What causes it?
- Take a position … if a tree falls in the forest and nobody is there to hear it, does it really make a sound? What elements of sound are needed in order to argue your case?
- What is that ringing sound in my ears?
- What are cochlear implants and how do they work?
- How do hearing aids work?

Name: _____ Date: _____

STUDENT INQUIRY ACTIVITY **11** : SCHOOLWIDE SOUND AWARENESS FAIR

Topic: Sound—Capstone Activity

As a class service-learning project, plan and conduct a Schoolwide Sound Awareness Fair. The goal of this project should be to increase awareness of sound and its effects on our daily lives. A guiding principle for the project is in order, e.g., "In what ways might my/our findings benefit the school and community?" Sample projects may include: increased awareness of sound principles, e.g., content information regarding sound; safety considerations regarding sound; technology applications of sound; career-related aspects of sound, etc.

This project may be a natural extension of the inquiry projects from the previous lesson. Stress the importance of application and dispersal of what the students have learned throughout the study of sound. Explain that this is science in action. Obviously, you must carefully screen each student project for accuracy, relevance, and appropriateness.

A project of this magnitude calls for student sub-committees and parental involvement. Encourage students and parents to take an active role in formulating and enacting committee responsibilities, e.g., invite other classes, teachers, administrators, and community members; take the opportunity to promote the project and utilize the local media to help with this; secure facilities and a date that are compatible with the school district.

If applicable, look for a public area in which to display the findings of students. Perhaps bank lobbies, libraries, local businesses, etc., may serve as appropriate areas for displays.

Name: _____ Date: _____

EXTENSION IDEAS AND INTERDISCIPLINARY APPLICATIONS

Sound Effects

Encourage students to create sound effects tapes and CDs. Begin by listening to and observing pre-manufactured sound effects recordings. Create an electronic classroom sound effects library and maintain it throughout the year. At the end of the year, select and combine the very best sound effects and compile a class tape or CD to remain for use with future classes. Each year, a new CD or tape could be added.

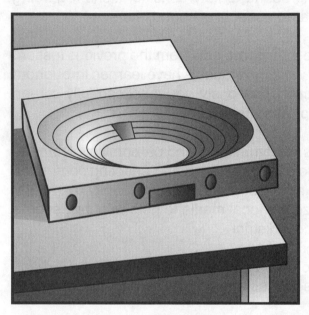

Building Design

Assume the role of a contractor who is in charge of building a theater in which musical concerts, operas, and plays will be held. What design factors should be accounted for, relative to optimum sound quality? Encourage students to build scale models of the theater, complete with the acoustics that would be desirable for such a facility.

Sound Maker

Choose a sound in nature and create a device (not a recording of the sound) to re-create the sound. For example, rain can be simulated using a heavy-duty Christmas wrapping paper tube, toothpicks, and rice. Drill small holes in the tube every centimeter along the line that wraps around the tube. The holes will spiral along the line. Insert and glue a toothpick into each hole; insert the toothpick all the way into the tube until it hits the other side. Glue where the toothpick enters the hole. After the glue has dried, use a fingernail clippers to trim off the excess portion of the toothpick. Be careful not to clip too close to the glued portion of the toothpick.

When viewed through the end, the tube should contain a series of toothpicks that appear to criss-cross each other inside the tube. Fill the tube roughly 1/3 full of rice. Cap both ends of the tube; a 35mm film canister lid and some tape work well. Decorate the outside of the tube to cover up the toothpick holes. One option is to wrap and glue various colors of string and/or thread. Masking tape would work as well.

Invert the tube and listen as the rice trickles down through the interior toothpicks. This activity can be reviewed in detail as it appears in Project W.E.T. (See reference list at end of book.)

Noise or Sound?

What is the difference? What is noise pollution, and why isn't it called sound pollution; or is it?

Voice Box Model

Build a model or diagram of the human voice box. Illustrate the main parts and their functions. Identify how speaking and hearing are related.

72

Name: _____ Date: _____

EXTENSION IDEAS AND INTERDISCIPLINARY APPLICATIONS (CONT.)

Electronic Sounds
Investigate how sounds are created, transmitted, and received in various technological devices used in communication. Compare and contrast earlier versions with more recent technology, e.g., reel-to-reel tape recorder and CDs; rotary telephones and cellular telephones.

Morse Code
Discover how sounds using Morse Code helped people to communicate.

Sign Language
Invite a sign language interpreter to provide basic sign language instruction. Discuss and analyze various hearing impairments and the special needs of this group of people. In what ways can hearing people be of assistance to those with hearing impairments?

Storm Sounds
Investigate the relationship between thunder and lightning. Can we determine the distance of a lightning strike using sound? Explain.

Sound Assistants
Offer to help a lower-grade-level class with the study of sounds and hearing, particularly as they study the five senses. Many kindergarten classes study the five senses and how we become more aware of our surroundings.

Mach What?
Research to find what is meant by Mach 10, Mach 3, Mach 18, etc. What is the sound barrier, and in what contexts is it broken?

Sounds and Space
Encourage students to apply the knowledge learned about sounds as they speculate about what happens to sounds as a rocket enters outer space. In what ways are astronauts able to hear sounds as they communicate with mission control?

73

BOOKS ABOUT SOUND

AUTHOR	TITLE	PUBLISHER	ISBN #
Ardley, Neil	*Sound and Music*	Franklin Watts	0-86313-159-X
Ardley, Neil	*The Science Book of Sound*	Harcourt Brace Jovanovich	015200579X
Baer, Gene	*Thump, Thump, Rat-a-Tat-Tat*	Harper Collins	0-440-83288-8
Baker, Wendy/ Haslam, Andrew	*Sound: A Creative, Hands-On Approach to Science*	Aladdin Books	0-689-71665-6
Baxter, Nicola	*Sound not Silence*	Children's Press	0-516-09269-3
Becker, Bonny	*The Quiet Way Home*	Henry Holt and Company	0-8050-3530-3
Behrens, June	*What I Hear*	Children's Press	0-516-08745-2
Blanchard, Arlene	*Sounds My Feet Make*	Random House	0-394-89648-3
Brandt, Keith	*Sound*	Troll Associates	0-8167-0129-6
Brinton, Henry	*Sound*	The John Day Company	
Cash, Terry/ Taylor, Barbara	*Sound*	Warwick Press	0-531-19064-1
Catherall, Ed	*Exploring Sound*	Raintree/ Steck-Vaughn	0-8114-2592-4
Cobb, Vicki	*Bangs and Twangs*	The Millbrook Press	0-7613-1571-3
Cole, Joanna	*The Magic School Bus in the Haunted Museum: A Book About Sound*	Scholastic Trade	059048125
Davies, Kay/ Oldfield, Wendy	*Sound and Music (Starting Science Series)*	Raintree/ Steck-Vaughn	0-8114-3003-0
De Pinna, Simon	*Sound*	Raintree/ Steck-Vaughn	0-8172-4944-3
Efron, Alexander	*Sound*	John F. Rider Publisher, Inc.	
Friedhoffer, Robert	*Sound*	Franklin Watts	0-531-11083-4
Gardner, Robert	*Experimenting with Sound*	Franklin Watts	0-531-12503-3
Gardner, Robert	*Science Projects about Sound*	Enslow Publishers	0-7660-1166-6
Gibson, Gary	*Hearing Sounds (Science for Fun)*	Copper Beech Books	1562946323
Hewitt, Sally	*Hearing Sounds*	Children's Press	0-516-20841-1
Kaner, Etta	*Sound Science*	Addison-Wesley Publishing Company	0-201-56758-X
Levine, Shar/ Johnstone, Leslie	*The Science of Sound and Music*	Sterling Publishing Co.	0-8069-7183-5
Marson, Ron	*Sound: Task Card Series*	TOPS Learning Systems	0-941008-88-6
Miller, Lisa	*Sound*	Coward-McCann, Inc.	

BOOKS ABOUT SOUND (CONT.)

AUTHOR	TITLE	PUBLISHER	ISBN #
Nankivell-Aston, Sally/Jackson, Dorothy	*Science Experiments with Sound*	Franklin Watts	0-531-15431-9
Neal, Charles D.	*Sound*	Follet Publishing Company	
Oxlade, Chris	*Science Magic with Sound*	Barron's	0812064461
Parsons, Alexandra	*Sound*	World Book	0-7166-4705-2
Parsons, Alexandra	*Sound*	Thomson Learning	1568474717
Peacock, Graham	*Sound*	Thomson Learning	1568470746
Ramsay, Helena	*Sound*	Children's Press	0-516-20958-2
Raschka, Christopher	*Charlie Parker Played Bebop*	Orchard Books	0531085996
Richards, Jon	*Sound and Music*	Copper Beech Books	0-7613-3254-5
Robinson, Fay	*Sound All Around*	Children's Press	0516460242
Rowe, Julian	*Making Sounds*	Children's Press	0516081365
Showers, Paul	*The Listening Walk*	Harper Collins	0060216387
Sootin, Harry	*Science Experiments with Sound*	W.W. Norton & Company	
Taylor, Barbara	*Sound and Music*	Warwick Press	0-531-19090-0
Taylor, Barbara	*Hear! Hear!*	Random House	0-679-80813-2
Walker, Colin	*Sound*	Modern Curriculum Press, Inc.	0-8136-7284-8
Ward, Alan	*Experimenting with Sound*	Chelsea House Publishers	0-7910-1511-4
Ward, Alan	*Sound and Music*	Franklin Watts	0-531-14237-X
Webb, Angela	*Talk About Sound*	Franklin Watts	0-531-10456-7
Williams, Vera	*Music, Music for Everyone*	Greenwillow Books	0688026044
Wise Brown, Margaret	*Noisy*	Harper & Row	
Wise Brown, Margaret	*The Quiet Noisy Book*	Harper Trophy	0-06-443215-7
Wise Brown, Margaret	*The Indoor Noisy Book*	Harper Collins	0-06-020821-X
Wise Brown, Margaret	*Noisy Book*	E.M. Hale and Company	
Wise Brown, Margaret	*Bunny's Noisy Book*	Hyperion Books for Children	0-7868-2428-X
Wood, Robert W.	*Physics for Kids: 49 Easy Experiments with Acoustics*	TAB Books	0-8306-3392-8

CURRICULUM RESOURCES

DSM II Earth Science: Sound, Grades 3–5
*Delta Science Module
http://www.delta-education.com

Science & Technology for Children: Sound, Grade 3
National Science Resources Center
Carolina Biological Supply
2700 York Road
Burlington, NC 27215
800-334-5551
http://www.carolina.com/

Communication
Lawrence Hall of Science
University of California
Berkeley, CA 94720
http://www.lhs.berkeley.edu/gems/

Task Oriented Physical Science (TOPS)
10970 S. Mulino Road
Canby, OR 97013
888-773-9755
www.topscience.org

Physics of Sound Module
Full Option Science Series (FOSS)
Lawrence Hall of Science
University of California
Berkeley, CA 94720
http://www.lhs.berkeley.edu/FOSS/

CLASSROOM RESOURCES

Ward's Natural Science
5100 W. Henrietta Road
P.O. 92912
Rochester, NY 14692-9012
800-962-2660
www.wardsci.com

Frey Scientific
905 Hickory Lane
P.O. Box 8101
Mansfield, OH 44901-8101
800-225-FREY (3739)
www.freyscientific.com

RECOMMENDED WEBSITES

www.billnye.com

www.ktca.org/newtons/

www.brainpop.com (use science link; select sound)

www.howstuffworks.com (type in a specific device, e.g., hearing aid)

http://www.exploratorium.edu/ti/resources/sound.html (good links to additional resources)

http://www.pbs.org/wnet/soundandfury/ (documentary about cochlear implants)

http://www.pbs.org/wgbh/nova/barrier/ (documentary about sound barrier and sonic boom)

http://pbskids.org/zoom/too/

http://KidsHealth.org/kid/ (a tour of the ear and hearing process)

http://place.scholastic.com/magicschoolbus/games/sound/index.htm

http://faculty.washington.edu/chudler/chhearing.html

REFERENCES

Asimov, I. (1966). *Understanding Physics*. New York: Barnes & Noble

Baker, W. (1993). *Sound: A Creative, Hands-on Approach to Science*. New York: Aladdin Books.

Borgford, C., Champagne, A., Cuevas, M., Dumas, L., Lamb, W., Vonderbrink, S. (2001). *Physical Science*. Austin, Texas: Holt, Rinehart, Winston.

Bosak, S. (1991) *Science Is …* Richmond Hill, Ontario: Scholastic.

Brandt, K. (1985). *Sound*. Mahwah, NJ: Troll Associates.

Burne, D. (1994). *Animals: How They Work*. New York: Sterling Publishing Co.

Cooney, T., Pasachoff, J., Pasachoff, N. (1990). *Physical Science*. Glenview, Illinois: Scott Foresman.

REFERENCES (CONT.)

DiSpezio, M. (1999) *Awesome Experiments with Light and Sound.* New York: Sterling Publishing Co.

Freeman, I. (1990). *Physics Made Simple.* New York: Doubleday.

Friedel, A. (1997). *Teaching Children Science, An Inquiry Approach.* New York: McGraw Hill.

Levine, S. Johnstone, L. *Science Experiments with Sound and Music.* New York: Sterling Publishing Co.

Llamas, A. (1996). *Five Senses of the Animal World: Hearing.* New York: Chelsea House Publishers.

Neal, C. (1962). *Sound.* Chicago: Follett Publishing.

Papastavrou, V. (1993). *Whale.* London: Dorling Kindersley.

Taylor, B. (1990). *Sound and Music.* New York: Warwick Press.

Turk, J., and Turk, A. (1987). *Physical Science.* Philadelphia: Saunders College Publishing Co.

(1995) *Project W.E.T.* Bozeman, Montana: Western Regional Environmental Education Council.